WANTED MAN

WANTED MAN

THE FORGOTTEN STORY OF
AN AMERICAN OUTLAW

TAMSIN SPARGO

BLOOMSBURY

First published in Great Britain in 2004
This paperback edition published in 2005

Copyright © 2004 by Tamsin Spargo

The moral right of the author has been asserted

Bloomsbury Publishing Plc, 38 Soho Square, London W1D 3HB

A CIP catalogue record for this book
is available from the British Library

ISBN 0 7475 7707 2
9780747577072

10 9 8 7 6 5 4 3 2 1

Typeset by Hewer Text Ltd, Edinburgh
Printed in Great Britain by Clays Ltd, St Ives plc

All papers used by Bloomsbury Publishing are natural,
recyclable products made from wood grown in well-managed
forests. The manufacturing processes conform to the
environmental regulations of the country of origin

www.bloomsbury.com/tamsinspargo

CONTENTS

(Reproduced from the collection of the Library of Congress)

I AM STANDING at a photocopier in the Library of Congress, scanning the room. The readers sit hunched over documents, pencil in hand. Nobody is interested in what anyone else is doing. Each is locked into his or her own world and time. There are no briefcases or bags, diaries or mobile phones. The personal clutter that connects us to the outside world has been taken away at the door, to be stowed in a locker until we leave. We may have arrived with a laptop or a leaky ballpoint, but now we each have only a pencil, some lined paper and a numbered locker key. I am number thirty-five.

One of my fellow researchers protested that he felt like a new inmate being admitted to prison. I have to confess that I quite like it. It's liberating and reassuring all at once, almost a return to child-hood, or my childhood at least, when someone else held the keys and the purse strings, leaving me free to play. Here you don't have to worry about losing anything except, perhaps, a sense of time.

But today security is on my mind. On the ceiling small video cameras are fixed at regular intervals. I try to work out what areas they cover.

I hope I look calmer than I feel. How do I do this? Do I 'accidentally'

1

drop the photograph on the floor with some other papers, then palm it into my trouser pocket? If I keep close to the photocopier it may work. But what if they search your pockets when you leave?

I didn't check because, when I walked into the library, I had absolutely no intention of stealing. I was a respectable academic on her way to view a newly donated archive. Barely twenty minutes later, I'm contemplating theft and my body is telling me that this isn't idle day-dreaming. My heart is beating fast, my palms are sweating. Then, just as I realize that the clichés are true, I know that I won't do it.

I finish my photocopying, return the documents to the librarian, reclaim my belongings and leave. As I pass through security at the main entrance I notice they don't check pockets.

Half an hour later, I'm sitting in a café, despondent, as if I've failed a test. I hadn't wanted to steal a unique manuscript or even a rare book, just a cheaply produced nineteenth-century tintype photograph. And it probably wouldn't have been missed. There were a dozen others in the folder where I found it. The archive was not yet catalogued, and I had been allowed access as a special favour. Why had I stopped? Was it fear of being caught? Or of what I would do with the photograph if I got away with it?

It wouldn't have been my first theft, although it would only have been my second. As a child I stole an eraser from the village shop as a dare, egged on by bolder girls. It wasn't the eraser I wanted, of course, but their approval. When I got home, I was so racked with guilt that I buried it in the part of the garden we called the wilderness. I felt hot flashes of shame every time I entered the shop, and whenever I saw those girls. I had passed the initiation test, but I would never be part of the 'gang'. Now, although I had never wanted a material object as much as I wanted the photograph, my nerve had failed.

I first saw the photograph in a 1950s coffee-table book about the Wild West. Since childhood, I have had a special relationship with the American West. Like many children who grew up in the 1950s and 1960s, I believed the world of cowboys and indians, ranchers and outlaws was not only real but current. Forty years ago, every other television programme seemed to be a Western, and the world of *The Virginian* appeared every bit as real as the English countryside. It seemed a place of safety, its moral certitudes as snug as its log cabins and wigwams. I moved on to *The High Chaparral*, and later, with my friends, debated the relative charms of Hannibal Heyes and Kid Curry. Our adolescent West was wilder, freer and full of passionate possibilities. Men on horseback rode through our dreams as, we were sure, they would one day ride into our lives.

I had a special connection. The characters from films and television were figures in my own family history, as real to me as my grandparents. And I was sure that I too would one day live in this world of legendary men and women. While my friends tried to gallop bareback and carved 'Pete Duel RIP' into their desks, I dreamed about what I was sure was my own manifest destiny. My father, nearly sixty when I was born, was raised on a farm in Cornwall, but the stories he told me at bedtime transported me to a more alluring family home. In the late nineteenth century, many of the Spargo men had gone west to America to seek their fortune. A cousin found a new life as one of the 'muckrakers', writers who exposed the suffering and corruption beneath the gilded surface of American society. An uncle worked as a carpenter for Buffalo Bill and stayed in the New York hotel run by Colonel Tom Thumb. The kitchen table on which I wrote my homework was made by a man who had built a shooting range for Annie Oakley. My own grandfather worked in a hospital in New York where he met Sitting Bull, before returning to Cornwall to raise cattle and a family.

As I grew up, so did my passion for the West. I rushed to the cinema to see *Butch Cassidy and the Sundance Kid*, *Willie Boy*, even *Little Big Man*, and scanned the shelves of second-hand bookshops for faded coffee-table books about the world of chuck-wagons. I knew, deep down, that my West was mythical, that when Uncle William worked for Buffalo Bill, he was building the scenery for a dream. But myths, and dreams, when we believe in them, even with our fingers crossed, do shape our lives. What I was looking for in the history of the West was not the truth, but a way back to the lost world of possibilities – of security, of freedom and of passion – of my own childhood.

Many books on the West are full of photographs: formal portraits of lawmen, mug shots of convicts, and chilling pictures of dead outlaws held up for the camera by their killers. In most, the eyes of the living men and women seem as dead as the deceased. They gaze into a middle distance, for ever out of our reach. But there are exceptions. The man in the photograph I wanted is one.

His collar is slightly too tight and his hair roughly cropped. He is unshaven, his face is bruised, and although his eyes seem troubled, one corner of his mouth is lifting towards a smile. Although the photograph was taken over a hundred years ago, he looks shockingly modern. He looks alive. His name is Oliver Curtis Perry and from the moment I first saw his face, I was in the grip of a powerful obsession that was not in the least academic. I wanted his picture not for my files but for my bedside.

When I saw Oliver Perry's photograph, I fell, unknowingly, for a doubly wanted man. The photograph was originally carried in the pocket of Pinkerton detectives in a nationwide manhunt. To those who wanted to bring him to justice, he was a remarkable, ruthless criminal, but to many of his fellow Americans he was a romantic, daring outlaw. This man occupied the dreams and fantasies of a generation.

I was only the latest in a long line of women, and men, who had fallen for Oliver Perry. Yet today, apart from sketches of brief moments in his life, he is a forgotten man, his story lost. What drew so many people to him in his lifetime? Was it the same challenging, wounded look that compelled me so long after his death? And why, unlike other outlaws, has he been almost completely excised from history?

Years after I stopped believing that I would ride off into the sunset with an outlaw lover, I had found myself face to face with him. The photograph transported me from my adult world of history into an adolescent romance, and I wanted it like young girls want pictures of their film-star idols. When my nerve failed, I found myself back in the real world, alone.

Because he was an outlaw and I was an academic, stealing his photograph would have somehow connected us. Leaving it in the folder felt like a betrayal, a confirmation that we were separated by more than time.

I kept tracking him across New York State and beyond, in detective agency archives, in prison records and newspapers of his day, even unearthing his own writings, unread since his death. With his photograph always in my head, if not my pocket, I proved a better detective than I would be a thief.

In the end I discovered a man of greater complexity and power than the handsome outlaw I had been hunting. I found many clues to his appeal to the men and women of his day. I also found out the terrible reason why he had been forgotten.

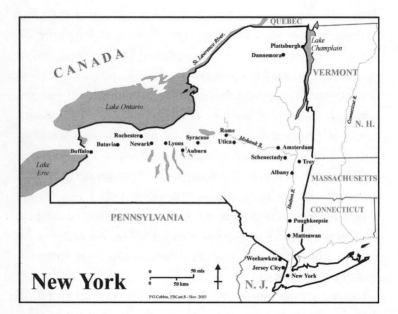

New York

QUEBEC
CANADA
Lake Ontario
Lake Erie
St. Lawrence River.
Plattsburgh
Dannemora
Lake Champlain
VERMONT
Connecticut R.
N. H.
Rochester
Rome
Batavia
Newark
Syracuse
Utica
Mohawk R.
Amsterdam
Buffalo
Lyons
Auburn
Schenectady
Troy
Albany
MASSACHUSETTS
Hudson R.
CONNECTICUT
PENNSYLVANIA
Poughkeepsie
Matteawan
Weehawken
Jersey City
New York
N. J.

0   50 mls
0   50 kms

P.G.Cubbin, FBCart.8 - Nov. 2003

CHAPTER I

Wild Western Ways
in the Empire State

I N M A R C H 1929 the thirty-first President of the United States
of America, Herbert Hoover, proclaimed: 'Ours is a land rich
in resources; stimulating in its glorious beauty; filled with millions
of happy homes; blessed with comfort and opportunity. In no
nation are the institutions of progress more advanced. In no
nation are the fruits of accomplishment more secure.' Just a few
months later, the stock market crashed and the happy nation
sank into depression and despair. In the hard years that followed
people would do almost anything to get by. On city streets men,
women and children queued for handouts and picked through
garbage to find food.

The city of Utica in central New York State's Mohawk valley was
as hard hit as any other. Once-booming businesses closed or laid off
most of their workers. Many Uticans who had come from other
lands, or from the surrounding countryside, searching for a better
life, moved on once more, in search now simply of work. Some
turned hobo, travelling along the railroad lines, risking the wrath of
the 'bulls' employed to keep the trains free of passengers who
would not or could not pay. An optimistic few, remembering tales
from their childhood, searched for better fortune nearer home.

Stories had been told about fantastic wealth, a robber's horde, buried in the Frankfort Hills, just outside the city, forty years before. So, armed with shovels and picks, Utica's Depression dreamers headed into the hills to dig. None succeeded, but their attempts to strike it rich in a world with no other hope echoed the actions of the man whose treasure they were seeking. Like them, he had hoped that one lucky break would transform his life of misfortune.

In the aftermath of the Civil War that convulsed the nation in the 1860s, America had entered an era of extraordinary economic growth. The technology of war, as ever, propelled the peacetime nation into a new age in which memories of loss mingled with hopes of gain. Steel, oil, copper, and the railroads needed to transport them, transformed the United States into one of the world's top three industrial powers. They also turned wartime speculators and profiteers into a new commercial aristocracy – J. Pierpont Morgan, John D. Rockefeller, Cornelius Vanderbilt, August Belmont – whose empires were centred on the Empire State. In New York City alone there were over a thousand millionaires by the 1890s. Their success seemed to be the ultimate fulfilment of an American dream, but real life for most Americans was in stark contrast.

Workers endured harsh, dangerous conditions, poor pay and no job security in industries that were almost entirely unregulated. Safety measures and decent wages were costly and, in a fiercely competitive free market, profit ruled. Exploited workers, in the mines and on the railroads, turned to desperate measures. Their strikes were, in turn, violently suppressed by hired strike breakers. Beneath the gilded surface of the age something very much like class war was simmering. Among the immigrants who arrived daily from the Old World were radicals, socialists and anarchists, determined, in different ways, to forge a better society. Their arguments found a growing working-class audience. Middle-class liberals, meanwhile, feared that the great industrialists were corrupting the system by routinely manipulating politicians for their own ends. In some circles a new name was found for them: 'the robber barons'.

In this competitive world, the fantasy of making it big fuelled a million schemes that fed on people's dreams. Every day a golden new business opportunity was advertised to take the citizen's dollar. Some were stranger than others. In Portland, Oregon a stock company was established to breed black domestic cats for fur. The company announced that an island would be purchased so that the stock could be isolated from other cats and live on fish. Prospective investors were assured that there were millions to be made in cats. For every dollar there was a waiting speculator. The spirit of the age was distilled by one commentator: 'Get money – honestly if you can, but at any rate get money!'

In New York State the post-war era had brought dramatic change. More and more people kept flooding into the state but the competition from more fertile agricultural lands in the west hit the upstate farmers hard. Rural workers soon began to give up and move to the towns to work in factories and mills. The booming cities of New York State were full of men and women, native-born and immigrant, who had grown up in close-knit communities but were now among strangers.

The landscape of the state still shows the effects of the industrial boom. The railroad travels north from New York City through the Hudson valley, then west along the Mohawk valley from Albany to Utica, and beyond to Rochester and Buffalo, tracing the ancient ways of the great rivers and the more recent routes of the industrial era. Cities are strung along the twin highways of water and rail, some named prosaically for their business, like Gloversville, others, like Amsterdam and Geneva, recalling the homes left behind by waves of immigrants. Still others speak of heroic identifications. The Empire State, even in its most mundane places, is overlaid with names from a classical mythology: Troy, Rome and Utica.

In 1891 Utica was a city of some standing, with new electric lights shining out across the dark surrounding hills. It was also the place where one of the most daring crimes in New York's history took place.

Late in the night of 29 September 1891 the New York Central 'American Express Special' set out from the state capital Albany on its long journey. The train, known to railroad buffs as 'the hottest of hotshots', travelled at top speed and carried no passengers. It was a vital link in the economic chain that connected businesses in the east and west of the nation, stopping to pick up freight along a route that finally led to Chicago. Like any freight train it was made up of cars owned by different companies. One of these was special. Outside, it looked just like any other, a wooden wagon with a solid door at each end and sliding panel doors with windows in the sides. But this was no ordinary freight car, carrying tinned goods or leather shoes.

It was owned by the American Express Company and was known by railroad workers as the 'money' car. It carried specie or cash from the United States Treasury for western banks, as well as bonds, jewellery and other valuables. Inside it was divided by crossways partitions into three compartments. In the central one, which held all the valuables in four large safes and numerous sacks, travelled an American Express employee called, innocuously enough, a 'messenger'. His job was to deal with all the paperwork for the company, but he was also an armed guard. The American Express Special, as it was popularly known, was reported to carry loads worth up to a million dollars.

Few messengers expected to use their regulation revolvers, on the eastern leg of the journey at least. Robberies had been a hazard in the wilder west since the first recorded train robbery in 1865. These were violent crimes, with trains derailed or blown apart and trainmen forced to defend their basic livelihoods with their lives. The names of the western outlaw gangs, Reno, James, Younger, were already legendary. Their methods were brutal but their origins in civil war conflict attracted the sympathy of some ex-Confederates and many romantics. A few radicals believed they were no more ruthless than the respectable 'robber barons' of the east. Men who made money fast, legally or illegally, inevitably did so at someone else's expense. Was a fast, bloody death in a western street or on a railroad track so much worse than a lifetime of dangerous drudgery in a factory or on a train? Whatever their thoughts about the comparative morality of bosses and outlaws, most easterners were relieved to know that daring train robbers belonged in another world, far away from 'civilized' New York.

But that September night everything changed. 'Wild Western Ways in the Empire State' declared the *New York Herald* the following morning, while Joseph Pulitzer's *The World* seemed geographically affronted: 'A train held up right in the heart of the Empire State! And this on one of the most frequented roads in the Union – the New York Central! It seems almost incredible that such wild Western methods could be successfully practised in the

11

centre of civilization without a trace being left as to the perpe-
trators of such a daring deed; yet such is a fact.'

The American Express Special was speeding though the 'burnt
stone' canyon, a few miles east of the bright lights of Utica, when
it suddenly ground to a halt. The trainmen, who travelled in the
last car, jumped down to investigate and found that someone had
cut through the air-brake hose at the rear of the money car. Inside
they found Burt Moore, the messenger, dazed and gasping, 'I've
been robbed.' The robbers had apparently disappeared in the
pitch darkness of the canyon. Unable to see well enough to give
chase, the crew travelled on to Utica to report the crime.

There the shocked messenger explained what had happened.
He was working in the central section, with the end doors locked.
The front partition door was open to make room for the freight,
and sacks and parcels were piled high against the front car door
because it would not be used on the journey. When the train
approached Frankfort, he was crouched with his back to this
door, checking the waybills that identified the sender, destination
and recipient of all the freight. The train was travelling at full
speed, engine roaring and cars clattering over the switches. Once
or twice he thought he heard something and looked around but
everything seemed in order, and his revolver was near at hand, on
top of a trunk.

Suddenly he heard a louder noise, turned and saw a man
pointing two guns at him. His face was completely covered by a
red hood, except for slots through which his eyes flashed. 'It's
money I'm after,' he shouted. 'Quick, we're getting near to Utica!'

Moore claimed that before he could react, a shot whistled past
him, and the robber grabbed his revolver. The masked man made
him unlock a safe, then emptied it, tossing aside bags of jewellery,

and stuffed half a dozen canvas bags into a large bag he carried over his shoulder. Keeping his guns trained on Moore, he moved slowly towards the side door and opened it as if to jump. But the train was travelling too fast and he changed his mind, backing towards the front door. Slowly, he felt his way back through the piles of packages and, keeping one gun stretched in front, dropped the bag through a square hole in the door, then wriggled, one foot at a time, back through the hole and dropped out of sight. Moore assumed that he had swung down to cut the brake hose that ran underneath the cars, to stop the train and make his escape. Whatever he did, he disappeared without trace.

The car itself told the story of how the robber had entered it. Standing on the platform as the train sped noisily through the night, he had bored a small hole in the front door, to spy on the messenger, then made four more holes lower down, and sawn out a panel, about fifteen inches square. Then he had leaned through, pulled out a box to stand on, squeezed into the car and surprised the messenger. It was a devastatingly simple plan, brilliantly executed. Unlike his western predecessors, this man had worked alone, and had used skill rather than brute force. He had also chosen to rob a train in the busiest state in the Union.

The police immediately cabled American Express and the railroad company. The robbery was a real embarrassment to both – and a threat to future profits. They swiftly announced that the train had been carrying an unusually small amount of money, less than $20,000 in total, and that mostly bonds. While all those interviewed, including New York Central Railroad President Chauncy M. Depew, acknowledged it was 'a queer case', they immediately insisted that little could have been stolen. American Express announced that the robber had stolen less than $1,000, and one official, stretching credulity to breaking-point, argued that it was only $150. Newsmen were sceptical. One consulted an Albany banker who confirmed the general view that the train was more likely to have carried at least $100,000.

American Express lost no time in employing the Pinkerton Detective Agency to find the robber. The agency had, like the corporations it now worked for, been 'made' by the Civil War, when its agents worked undercover for the Union side, and was known for getting results by any means necessary. Now the 'Pinks', under the direction of Robert Pinkerton himself and the agency's New York manager, George Bangs, assembled in Utica. There they joined a throng of railroad detectives, local police and newsmen and started the painstaking process of searching the surrounding towns, villages and countryside. It was the biggest manhunt upstate New York had seen for many years.

The Pinkertons had years of experience in dealing with train robberies in the west, where a network of detectives, local sheriffs and informers had given them real success. But this was a challenge. The man they were after was clearly no ordinary robber. George Bangs, a man not easily impressed, wrote to William Pinkerton, 'The man who committed the train robbery here is one of the nerviest I ever heard of. There are few if any men who possess the daredevil courage to accomplish what this train robber did yesterday.' And as the days passed no trace of the robber came to light, nor any clue to his identity.

Then, five days after the crime, a couple of local men made an important discovery while picking ink-berries in Borden's Grove. This was a patch of scrubland near an abandoned distillery, some three miles east of Utica. They were about to call it a day and go home, when they spotted a lot of torn paper on the ground. On closer inspection, the paper turned out to be wrappers from money and bonds. Nearby were empty money envelopes, packages and jewellery boxes as well as large cotton bags with the marking 'Am. Ex. Co.'. Among the papers they found a waybill listing 'three diamond rings' and an envelope marked '$5,000'.

They bundled everything up and went to find a local reporter who immediately set off on the trail of the robber. Just behind the place where the wrappings had been found was a deep, over-grown ravine that ran south from the canal into the Frankfort Hills. Full of stubby trees and bushes, it offered ideal hiding places. The reporter drove along the road until he found what he was looking for: someone who had a story to tell.

Erving Vance, a farmer, was not an ideal witness. Until an apparently miraculous but mysterious 'cure', he had been totally blind. His sight had been only partially restored, however, and he had to rely on his ten-year-old son to help him on the farm. On the evening after the robbery, he had gone out to bring a horse into the barn for the night, taking his son with him. As he approached the barn he saw an object looming in the semi-darkness and assumed it was the horse, but the object said, 'Good evening.' 'Well, what do you want?' Vance had replied, startled. The stranger had answered that he was looking for Mr Rider's place. 'Holmes Rider?' asked the farmer. 'Yes,' came the answer.

Suspicious of anyone prowling around his farm, Vance had asked who he was. According to the farmer, at this point the man started to behave as if he was slightly drunk. He said he had been drinking with two friends, had fallen asleep on the road, and woken to find they had gone. As far as Vance could make out, the man had said his name was Stevens or Stevenson, and he came from Little Falls, but had worked in Amsterdam for a time before that. He had seemed increasingly uneasy and anxious to leave. Told the way to Rider's farm, he started off in another direction until Vance called out. After some hesitation he changed his path and the farmer and son, who knew nothing about the train robbery, watched him disappear into the darkness.

Vance gave the reporter a description that, although lacking in detail because of his impaired vision, matched that of the train robber given by Burt Moore: about five feet nine, of rather slight build, with a small dark moustache. His son confirmed his story and other sightings followed. A bee hunter remembered seeing a man who kept his face hidden and who, if a local barber was to be believed, made his way back to Utica that evening, walked into the barber's shop and asked to have his moustache shaved off. The man's clothes, the barber said, were dusty and covered with 'stick tights' or burrs, and he clutched a newspaper-covered parcel. He had paid from a 'good roll of bills' and left. After that the trail went cold. But the reporter's search had uncovered two things about the robber. The fact that he had named a local farmer suggested that the robber might be a local man. The fact that he had coolly walked back into Utica, under the detectives' noses, confident that he would not be identified, showed that he was as daring as a wanted man as he had been as a robber.

The Borden's Grove find had also proved something else: that whatever American Express said, this had been a major robbery. Someone leaked the fact to a reporter that four more canvas bags and their contents had not been accounted for and the remaining empty bags were soon found on top of an eastbound freight car near Albany. Whatever the official line, the growing band of newspapermen in Utica knew they were on to a real story and the public were eager for the latest chapter.

If American Express was under pressure, the crew of the robbed train had reason to feel even more uncomfortable. Many people insisted that the robber must have had inside knowledge or help, and the police were searching for one suspect, an escaped convict, just because he had been a railroad worker. The most worried man was messenger Burt Moore. Although he had been in shock after the robbery, he had not been hurt. To some observers this was deeply suspicious. He was a powerfully built man who did not appear to have put up much of a fight. It was also rumoured that no evidence could be found that any shot had been fired in the car. Possibly Moore had invented the shooting because he was worried his employers would not think he had put up enough of a fight, but as time went on, some whispered that he had been in cahoots with the robber. Moore was anxious to show that he had done everything he could to protect his employer's goods, even claiming that he had managed to hide some money by kicking a sack of bills out of sight while the robber was distracted. His employers announced that they had total faith in him, but he had been immediately suspended from duty after the robbery and was under continual surveillance.

A week after the Borden's Grove find and nearly a fortnight after the robbery, American Express issued an official statement: 'We have got a pretty good clue to the robber and we are going to get him. It may take time, but we will run him down if we have to follow him to "Kingdom Come" . . . Watch us while we nab the robber.' So watch the people of New York did, for weeks on end. But still there was no arrest.

Pinkerton Detective Agency Flyer.

CHAPTER 2

'Probably now wearing diamonds'

WHILE THE people of New York wondered if the Pin-kertons had finally met their match, the detectives believed they had found their man. They had started to follow a lead from one of the train's crew, Frank Stacy. He had caught a glimpse of the robber as he jumped from the train and thought he recognized him as a one-time colleague on the New York Central. For the first time, the wanted man had a name: Oliver Curtis Perry.

The Pinkertons at first revealed nothing to the police or the press. They started by targeting the suspect's relatives, particularly his aunt, a respectable woman called Mary Hamblin, who lived in the nearby city of Rome. Agents offered her $250, a substantial sum, for a photograph of her nephew but she refused to cooperate. Eventually they had a warrant issued against her and obtained a copy of the photograph for use in their circulars. These were sent all over the country, offering a huge reward of $1,000.

The circulars gave a description that echoed those given by Burt Moore and the local witnesses, but was clearly based on detailed knowledge of the suspect:

Oliver Curtis Perry is described as 26 years of age, 5 feet 6 to 7 inches in height, slight build, weighing about 130lbs, dark brown hair, small moustache, inclined to be sandy (probably now shaved off), brown eyes; high, white forehead, with wrinkles between eyes, giving his face a troubled and thoughtful expression; thin lips, rather long nose, slim white hand, with enlarged knuckles from hard work. Has a scar about three inches long on upper part of forehead, which is noticeable when his hat is off; also has scar on left arm and above right nipple. He is gentlemanly, polite and effeminate in manner, but acts nervous and uneasy; has a girlish voice, dresses in dark clothes, invariably wears gloves, and is noticeably particular about keeping his hands clean. Had gold open face watch, 14 karat, stemwinder, size 18, Samuel C. Tappen, Troy, N.Y., maker, name on dial and movement, nickel movement, case No. 14,608; also a gold watch chain. Also wears a ring, with stone on little finger of right hand, (probably now wearing diamonds).

The photograph shows a handsome man with dark eyes, gazing calmly past the photographer. He is dressed like a respectable gentleman but not a man of means. The fabric of his suit looks, on close inspection, to be coarse. He may, like many Americans of the period, have taken advantage of the cheap 'smart' clothes designed to make a hick pass without being mocked in the city, or a worker feel like a boss, if only on Sundays. But he was clearly a man of refined tastes: his cravat looks like silk and has a sprig of flowers on the knot. His hair is sleek and his moustache is slightly curled at the ends. A comment under the picture warns the viewer: 'The above likeness is a good one but flatters. His face is not so full and the lips are thinner.'

The flyers gave a wealth of detail about the robber's looks, but what about his character? Who was Oliver Perry? While the hunt continued, two wildly contrasting versions emerged as the press fed the public appetite for information on him. The Pinkertons declared that he was a clever but ruthless outlaw. According to them he was born, as many had suspected, in the Mohawk valley, and had a long record of crimes across the States. But for the past two years Perry had been working on the railroad and living quietly in Troy, a city near Albany, some of whose most upstanding citizens sprang to his defence. They insisted that Perry was a man of strong religious convictions who had seen the error of a wayward youth, and tried to keep to a steady path until this extraordinary allegation had been made. These were eminently respectable people, and their loyalty to the fugitive surprised the detectives. One, the City Missionary and Sunday School teacher, Miss Amelia Haswell, protected him even more ferociously than his aunt had done, destroying his photographs rather than have them used on reward posters. Oliver Perry clearly inspired strong passions.

The agents redoubled their efforts, with William A. Pinkerton himself leading investigations across the continent. Detectives searched hotels and brothels, Christian associations and saloons; they even arrested a man in Vermont and announced their hunt was over, only to discover it was a case of mistaken identity. Perry was not to be found. In the press speculation continued about whether or not he had worked entirely alone. The fact that he had been a railroad worker had explained his inside knowledge of trains but it was over two months since the robbery and Burt Moore had still not been allowed back to work. Could he have been an accomplice?

Then, in December, two strange things happened. First, a lawyer from Troy delivered a parcel of jewellery stolen in the robbery to American Express. The Pinkertons questioned Perry's religious friends, but revealed nothing to the press. Next, an astonishing letter, postmarked 'Guelph Ontario', arrived at the investigation headquarters. Its exact contents were not revealed, but it was signed 'Oliver Curtis Perry' and accompanied by a diamond-studded brooch from the Special, to prove its authenticity. Its writer made a full confession, and insisted that Burt Moore was totally innocent. Perry, it seemed, had recklessly revealed his whereabouts in order to prevent an injustice. Agents in Ontario were alerted, but again they failed to find him. To those of a romantic inclination the letter was an act of gallantry, designed to save a working man from more trouble, while others were amused by Perry's ability to tease the detectives.

New Year came, still there was no sign of an arrest, and still the robber's reputation grew. Anyone who had got away with a fortune as he had would have earned the secret admiration of all but the most determinedly upright: his robbery was quite simply astonishing. But there was something about Oliver Perry, sketchily as he had been drawn, that particularly caught the imagination of New Yorkers. The references to his troubled expression and nervous manner had suggested to some that this was a daredevil with a sensitive soul. The comments from the good people of Troy had, after all, painted a picture of a hard-working man and his letter had shown he was honourable. And, despite the Pinkertons' snide remark, everyone could see that he was handsome. Perry became the object of the day-dreams and fantasies of men, women and children: a man you might want to be, or be with, or become.

Soon rumours spread across the state that poor people were finding jewels and money on their doorsteps with notes from Perry giving his compliments. Although there was never any proof that these incidents actually occurred, they fed a mythology that was growing around the young robber. Handsome, boyish, clever and honourable, he now became for some people a latter-day Robin Hood, a worthy successor to Jesse James, an eastern outlaw to rival any the west could boast. Did he, like them, have a dramatic past to explain his criminal present? In the coming months and years, tall tales would be spun about what Perry did on the run: stories of romantic assignations with beautiful women, of cool conversations about the robbery with unsuspecting detectives, and of secret caches of loot left deep in the Utica Hills to be recovered one day. Whatever the truth about Oliver Perry might turn out to be, New York had fallen in love.

CHAPTER 3

Shades of Jesse James!

I T W A S 20 February 1892. The American Express Special was once again making its run with the extra-valuable Saturday load. In the money car, messenger Daniel McInerney settled down to his paperwork. In the early hours of the morning, as the train pulled out of Syracuse, where it had stopped to take on freight, a smartly dressed, bearded man leapt unseen on to the forward platform of the car in front of McInerney's. Once aboard, he removed his gold-framed spectacles and placed them in the inside pocket of his overcoat. Then he climbed on to the platform railing, grasped the edges of the two cars and hauled himself up on to the roof.

Crouching low and keeping to the middle, he ran along the roof to the other end and dropped down on to the rear platform. From there it was just a step to the front platform of the car he was interested in, the money car. The speed of the train, as it left the depot, had forced him to jump aboard the wrong car. The run along the roof had not been part of his plan but he had managed it without even taking off his hat.

Once safely on the platform, he removed the derby and, threading a cord through the sweatband, strapped it to the railing, with his valise. The man who had got away with a fortune from American Express was robbing the same train again just five months later.

From his satchel Perry took a red hood with eye and mouth holes, which he tied tightly around his neck. It was the same mask he had used last time. Why change a winning formula? He strapped his Colt .44 and cartridge belt across his overcoat. The revolver was cumbersome, with a seven-inch barrel and a bore you could put your finger in but it had an impact as big as its pull. He placed two smaller revolvers, Derringers, in his coat pockets, within easy reach in case he dropped the larger gun. Given what he was about to do, that was a distinct possibility.

He levered himself up once again, this time on to the roof of the money car. From his satchel he took a rope with a hook at one end and knots at intervals along its length. He attached the hook to the overhanging eave on one side of the car. Then, keeping the rope taut, he stretched it across the roof and dropped it over the other side. It slipped down beside the door. Unlike the solid end door, this had a glass window. Perry leaned down, listening for any sign that he had disturbed the messenger inside, then inched down the rope.

The train was now travelling at nearly fifty miles an hour. A slip would be fatal. Perry wrapped his legs around the rope, to leave his hands free. The wind was so strong that the rope was blown away from the car several times, once nearly crashing into a bridge as the train hurtled under it. Seeing it just in time, in the lights of the train, Perry grasped the roof ledge and pulled himself towards the train. He missed death by inches.

He had to move quickly as well as carefully. The biting wind was almost unendurable. Wearing only fine kid gloves, his hands were becoming numb. He slapped them against his sides to keep his circulation going, then made his move.

Half an hour after the train pulled out of Syracuse, Daniel McInerney was startled by the sound of breaking glass. Grabbing his gun, he turned to see a revolver poking through the smashed window in the door. Just as he caught a glimpse of a masked head framed in the window, a voice called out, 'Hands up!'

A split second later both men fired at once. A bullet hit McInerney's gun and sent it flying back over his shoulder, breaking his fingers and smashing his wrist as it flew. With his good hand, he grabbed the air-whistle cord above his head and pulled it hard. No whistle sounded. He pulled again. 'Let go of that rope, damn you!' shouted the stranger. McInerney kicked out wildly to extinguish the lamp, plunging the car into darkness. A shot rang out and a bullet grazed his temple.

Dazed by the blow, he could hear the intruder climbing into the car and struggled desperately to pull the cord again. This time a third shot hit him in the thigh and floored him. The whole exchange had taken only seconds.

Too shocked to register much pain, McInerney could feel blood oozing from his leg. Perry struck a match and lit some waybills. In the light of the burning papers McInerney caught the full effect of the red mask and the two heavy revolvers. 'Damn you!' shouted Perry. 'You tried to kill me.'

Perry ordered McInerney to light the lantern, unlock the safes and put the money on one side. 'There is no money,' McInerney replied. Taken aback, Perry demanded that the messenger open the packages he had pulled out on to the floor. Sure enough, there was no cash, only jewellery and silverware. This wasn't right. He only wanted ready money this time, not goods that had to be sold.

McInerney insisted that the money was being carried on another train. Perry didn't believe him and ordered him to start opening up the other packages.

Emil Laas, the conductor travelling in the rear car, thought he heard the air-whistle sound faintly. When he went to see if anything was wrong in the money car, he peered through a hole and saw the strange hooded figure. He signalled quickly to the engineer to slow down but the masked head emerged from the side window and shouted, 'God damn you, shove her ahead!' A bullet whizzed past and the conductor complied.

As the train steamed on, Perry was still trying to find the money, but he started to worry about McInerney who was losing a lot of blood and showing real pain now. 'Are you hurt much?' he asked. Then he leaned forward to examine the messenger's wounded face by the light of some burning waybills. But as he got close, he saw McInerney staring at him and pulled back. Even with the mask, he couldn't let the other man look too closely. It was too risky.

Then, as the train approached Port Byron, it started slowing down. The engine had been signalled to halt to let a coal train pass. As Laas jumped off and called for the station operator, McInerney appeared at the car door, swaying and mumbling incoherently. There was no sign of the masked man. He must, Laas thought, have jumped off the train before it had picked up speed.

In fact, as they slowed down at Port Byron Perry had silently swung up on to the car roof and packed the rope away in his satchel. Then he dropped off the train on the side away from the trainmen just before it stopped. He hid while the train was being searched and gathered his thoughts. A freight train, bound for

Syracuse, was pulling out. Reckoning that he would be expected to try to get away on the freight train, he decided on a different course of action. He stowed away his disguise and other gear in his valise, and put on his hat and eyeglasses. Then he climbed back aboard the Express just before it set off for the next stop, the village of Lyons, and hid between cars.

When the train arrived in Lyons, McInerney was carried off for medical attention and the train was backed up on the number two track to take on water. Even though a messenger was seriously, perhaps fatally, wounded, the train would have to continue on to its destination as it had in the last robbery. When profits might be lost, the demands of the business outweighed the needs of its employees. Perry, meanwhile, slipped off on the far side, away from the platform, and walked swiftly along the track. Keeping hidden behind stationary train cars, he made his way to the street running up to the station. Then, cool as can be, he sauntered on to the platform as if coming to buy a ticket or meet a passenger. But his disguise, so often his best weapon, now proved his undoing.

While his train was refuelled, Emil Laas was discussing the robbery with the other railroad men, when he had his second shock of the night. At the far end, leaning casually against the station building, he saw a well-dressed young man he had noticed at the depot in Syracuse earlier that night. He hadn't thought much of it at the time, but this didn't make sense. There was no way the man could have got to Lyons that quickly except on the Express. The man had to be the robber. He shouted to the others. They rushed at Perry, then stopped in their tracks when he levelled his revolvers at them and ordered them to stay away.

Keeping the guns trained on the men on the platform, Perry backed slowly across the tracks. A west-bound coal train was standing on track number three, waiting for the signal to pull out. He swiftly uncoupled the engine from the rest of the train. Then he climbed over the water tank and ordered the startled engineer and fireman off the cab at gunpoint. As the men on the platform looked on in disbelief, Perry pulled open the throttle like a seasoned engineer and gave four whistle blows to signal departure. Hearing the whistle, the flagman, unaware of the unfolding drama, signalled the okay and Perry's engine pulled out of the station. Laas and the others were momentarily stunned but swiftly set off after Perry in the uncoupled Express engine. One of the men had hastily grabbed a double-barrelled shotgun.

As they raced through the quiet of the early morning, the Express quickly gained ground on Perry's 'hog', as the older, slower freight engines were known. Near a bridge over the Erie Canal, halfway along the ten-mile stretch between Lyons and Newark to the west, Perry saw that he had no hope of outrunning his pursuers. He slammed on the brakes, threw his engine into reverse, and built up speed until the engine hurtled backwards towards the Express. Perry was turning a race he couldn't win into a duel. Bullets flew as the engines chased and faced each other until, out of ammunition and reluctant to tackle Perry unarmed, the trainmen returned to Lyons. Behind them, their quarry-turned-opponent steamed away towards Newark.

But Perry had been too busy changing direction and shooting at his pursuers to keep the engine stoked, so the steam started to give out. He might have struggled into Newark but he knew that

The Engine Duel (*Utica Saturday Globe*).

the railroad men would have wired ahead and arranged a welcome party. So he abandoned the engine at Blue Cut, a couple of miles east, where he ordered a startled switchman to take the engine back to Lyons, and scrambled quickly up the embankment. When he reached the top, he looked around to see if anyone was watching, then set off into the countryside. Escape would not be easy. Heavy snowdrifts would make the going hard and the advancing daylight would help his pursuers.

By this time, the Rochester police force had been wired and were assembled at Rochester's Central station where they awaited the Express's arrival. McInerney was taken by ambulance to his parents' house, then, after questioning the crew, the policemen climbed aboard a specially requisitioned engine and set off on the thirty-five-minute run to Blue Cut. They telegraphed to Newark to have some local men meet them, but when they arrived at the Cut, no one was there. The crew of a passing freight train claimed to have seen Perry a short distance further east, so the police set off in that direction.

After struggling through the snow for some minutes, Perry spotted a farmhouse. Samuel Goetzman was in his kitchen having breakfast when there was a knock at his door. The caller, his face blackened by soot and sweat, told the farmer that he was a Pinkerton detective. He said he was chasing three men who had just robbed a train down on the Central and made off to the hills to the north. In order to pursue them he needed to borrow a horse.

Goetzman's first inclination was to shut the door. But after a great deal of persuasion, he reluctantly took the stranger to his barn. The man demanded to know which was his best horse. Goetzman pointed to a black mare. She was actually his second-best, but there was no reason for the stranger to know that. He asked the detective how he could be sure the mare would be returned. Perry was starting to explain that if anything happened to the horse he could sue American Express for compensation, when the farmer's wife walked in on them. When she realized what was happening, she flatly instructed her husband not to lend the stranger the horse. The mare happened to be her favourite, and if her husband was stupid enough to trust a total stranger, she was not.

Caught between civic and marital obligations, Goetzman asked if the 'detective' would show him his papers. The man replied that he didn't have any, but that his name was Cross. When Goetzman shook his head and said he needed some proof, Perry finally lost his temper. He grabbed a bridle from a hook on the wall and started to put it on the mare. While Goetzman stared, his wife tried to snatch the bridle off the stranger. He pulled it free, fitted it, and started leading the mare out of the barn. If he was determined to have the horse, Mrs Goetzman was equally resolved that he should not. Shouting at her husband, she tried to wrest the reins from the so-called detective. Fearful of losing any more time, Perry changed tactics. He pulled a revolver from his belt and pointed it at the woman.

The move worked. Goetzman rushed to find a blanket and strapped it on the mare. Keeping up his pretence, Perry demanded to know which was the best road to cut off the robbers' escape. The farmer told him to ride to the Blue Cut and turn right. He watched as Perry rode off, then took off after him in his cutter, a type of sleigh. At Blue Cut he saw, by the tracks in the snow, that Perry had gone left instead of right. Convinced now that the stranger was no detective, Goetzman called the local watchman who joined the chase.

The police, meanwhile, had realized that they were on a wild goose chase and doubled back to Blue Cut. There they tried to find someone to lend them horses or a cutter, but the local farmers were wary of all strangers. The city lawmen were greeted with as much suspicion as the bogus detective. Eventually a farmer agreed to drive them and they set off south in the direction taken by Perry.

Perry himself rode hard through the icy morning, anxious to keep ahead of the men he knew would be following. The snow had arrived about ten weeks earlier and few had travelled these roads since, as bare rock giving way to deep snowdrifts made the way perilous for horse or man. Eventually, about four miles on, Goetzman's second-best horse began to tire. Perry pulled up at a farm owned by another immigrant farmer, a Swede by the name of Frederick Beal.

Beal was feeding his chickens when Perry rode into the yard. Assuming the stranger wanted to ride through his fields because the road was blocked with snow, Beal called out, 'You can't get through here, there's too much snow.'

'I don't intend to go through,' came the reply. 'I want one of your best horses, and one of the fastest, right off.'

Beal asked what he wanted it for. Perry told him that he needed a horse and cutter to go to the aid of some men who were hurt down on the railroad. Beal started to ask what had happened and who Perry was. Unwilling to go through a repeat performance of the Goetzman conversation, Perry reached for his gun and fired a warning shot. Beal hitched up the cutter. Perry grabbed the reins, turned the cutter around so fast that it nearly toppled over, and sped out of the yard.

Soon every farmer and lad in the area were chasing Perry along the narrow tracks, on horseback, in cutters, buggies and carts. Few knew about the train robbery, but horse theft was about the worst crime a man could commit in the eyes of a Wayne County farmer.

Each time the farmers began to gain on Perry, at an awkward corner or a deep drift of snow, a shot from his revolver would keep them at bay until he was out of danger. One young man, Charlie Burnett, earned a new reputation for daredevil courage. Fired up by the thrill of the chase, he determined to be the one to catch the thief. Twice he forced Perry to change direction by shouting to wagons coming towards them in the opposite direction to block the road, making the robber turn down smaller side roads. Finally, he managed to overtake him and, trying to over-turn his cutter by barging his horse against Perry's, forced him to turn abruptly into a log road that ran into Benton's swamp.

The combination of snow and half-frozen swamp water forced Perry to abandon the cutter after a few hundred yards. He struggled on, wading through the swamp, until he reached a scrubby wooded area at the far edge. Keeping a safe distance between themselves and Perry's guns, his pursuers discussed their next move. Behind the vanguard of angry farmers, three more groups had been advancing. First were the Rochester police in their commandeered cutter. Second was a large posse from Lyons. Third were local Pinkerton agents. Altogether, more than fifty men were now crowded at the edge of Benton's swamp.

It was about 11 o'clock. Perry had been on the run for at least five hours. Exhausted, numb with cold and now soaked to the skin, he found a half-collapsed stone wall. Unable to walk any further, he crouched down behind it. His pursuers had split up to surround him. Just before midday, someone spotted Perry. Knowing that the posse would eventually close in on him, he had built up the loose stones from the wall into a sort of fortress. He knew that although he still had some ammunition, he could not win in any shoot-out with so many men. His only hope was to keep them at bay until nightfall and then try to creep away unseen. It was a long shot. There were hours to go before it would get dark, and he thought he heard someone in the posse call out a request to send to Lyons for long-distance rifles. For what felt like an age to everyone, there was a tense stand-off. No shots were fired and it seemed that both sides were playing a waiting game, to be decided by which arrived first, the long-distance rifles or nightfall.

'Is there an officer in the crowd?' It was Perry's voice from behind the barricade. 'I am,' shouted back Jeremiah Collins, the young deputy, known to everyone as Jerry. 'If you drop your gun and come on unarmed I'll talk with you,' Perry replied, 'but if you try to play me any tricks it will go hard with you.'

Ignoring all the warnings that he would get himself shot, Deputy Collins laid down his gun and walked across the open swamp towards Perry's improvised fortress, his hands clasped behind his back. Perry kept his gun trained on the approaching Deputy. 'Stop and hold your hands in front of you where I can see them.' Collins did so and moved forward again until he was standing against the wall in front of Perry.

'Is the messenger alive?' was the first thing Perry said. In the car he had been genuinely concerned about McInerney, who was about the same age and build as him, no tough guy. His plan had been to 'get the drop' on him, shock him into surrendering his gun, not have a shoot-out. But now he needed to know for another reason. If McInerney was dead or dying and he was facing a murder charge, there might be little reason to give himself up.

Collins said the messenger was alive and asked Perry to point the muzzle of the gun away from him. Perry hesitated, then laid it on the wall.

'You might as well give in,' Collins said, 'the whole country is out after you and you are bound to be caught. Suppose you do kill a few people. It'll only be worse for you in the end.'

'If I give up,' replied Perry, 'it means spending all my life in prison. Liberty is sweet to me and I'll sell it dear.'

Then, hearing a noise behind him, he turned around to check, and at that moment Collins took his chance. He knocked the pistol off the wall into the snow and launched himself across the wall, grabbing Perry in a bear-hug. Perry struggled and managed to unbalance Collins. The two men fell to the ground fighting.

Eventually Collins pinned him down on his back. Perry kept struggling. His arms held down, he tried to bite Collins's face, but the Deputy had size on his side. The watching men, bolder now, moved in as Collins handcuffed his captive and prepared to take him back to jail. Slowly the crowd dispersed. Some returned to their farms and chores they had left undone. More followed the posse back to Lyons to witness the next scene in the drama.

Perry had done the unthinkable. After single-handedly robbing the American Express Special and evading capture for over four months he had, everyone assumed, got away with his crime and a fortune. Now he had risked everything, including his freedom, by trying to rob the very same train again. Why had he done it? This robbery had been as meticulously planned as the first but the decision to do it was extraordinary. Was he showing off, inviting capture, or both? What sort of man would be so bold, so rash? America's most wanted man had been captured, but just who was Oliver Perry?

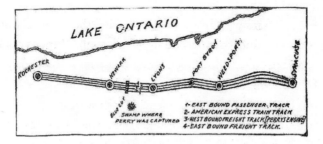

The scene of the robbery and chase

CHAPTER 4

'Woman's Mawkish Sentimentalism Again Manifests Itself'

THE WAYNE County Jail in Lyons is an attractive building on the outside. Standing on Butternut Street, in the chocolate-box pretty centre of the village, it looks like a sturdy family house. Until not long ago it was just that, housing the sheriff and his family, as well as local wrongdoers in separate quarters. Today it

Wayne County Jail (From the collection of
the Wayne County Historical Society, Lyons, New York).

is a museum. The family quarters display civil war memorabilia, regional crafts and work by local schoolchildren, symbols of a close-knit community, past and present. On the ground floor a small room serves as office and shop. At the back of this is a stout door behind which is the one part of the jail that has no modern use: the cellblock.

When word spread that the captive was Oliver Curtis Perry, the notorious train robber, reporters, policemen, detectives, treasure hunters and curious members of the public descended on Lyons in droves. Almost as quickly, keen entrepreneurs started hawking a suspiciously large supply of bent bullets and shards of glass among the crowds as genuine souvenirs of the engine duel.

While the people of Lyons stood outside the jail hoping to catch a glimpse of the man the press now declared had 'outdone' Jesse James, inside a crowd of policemen, detectives and even reporters had been granted access to identify the suspect. When they placed the exhausted robber in one of the small cells, the lawmen knew they had a real catch. All they needed was a formal identification as the prisoner insisted he was called William Cross and came from New Mexico. Perry must have been exhausted and should have been overwhelmed, but he impressed everyone with his cool manner and dry wit. One railroad detective who had encountered him years before asked if he knew who he was. 'Yes,' replied Perry, to the amusement of onlookers and the annoyance of the detective, 'but I never knew any good of you.'

When Perry had been formally identified, he dropped the false name that he may have hoped was a last chance of evading charges for the first robbery. Calmly and without apparent concern, he confirmed that he was indeed Oliver Curtis Perry, the son of Oliver H. Perry, a contractor from Syracuse, and confessed to the attempted robbery that day and to the successful robbery in 1891. Such was his apparent self-assurance that an agent for American Express who spoke with him in the jail told reporters, 'I never saw anyone who was so cool.' His coolness would be put to the test as he awaited his trial.

The jail itself was not daunting. Many prisoners preferred the regime of the county jail to the penitentiaries to which they might be sent after sentencing. The smaller jails had quite a homely atmosphere, and conditions, though tough, were rarely unduly harsh. Most prisoners were being held for minor offences, like drinking or fighting. Many knew their keepers. Like the lunatics in early Bedlams, however, the more infamous prisoners in jails were expected to be on display. Some guardians of law and order were happy to run their jails like sideshows, while others were more reluctant. But when more influential local citizens wanted to see the show, few sheriffs had the real power to refuse. The Wayne County Jail was no exception and soon Perry would have a stream of visitors. Among them were reporters with whom the young robber struck up a very special relationship.

Oliver Perry had a remarkable ability to make use of the press. From his earliest interviews in Lyons it is clear that he knew he was big news but also that he could manipulate public sentiment and spin a story for his own ends. Many years later he would quote President Theodore Roosevelt's comment that the quickest way to work for change was through the newspapers. Now he just seemed to have an almost instinctive understanding of how his gifts as a story-teller and talker might win him new friends. As he adjusted to his new situation, the man who had meticulously planned two robberies now embarked on a new project: to win over his audience. Public fascination with Perry had grown since his mysterious disappearance from Utica and he had followed the stories in the press that had fed this interest. Now he took the chance to tell his own tales. He started by explaining how he had evaded capture in Utica. His account pushed at the edge of credibility, especially an anecdote of hiding in a field where an unknowing farmer built up a corn stack around him, but the basic narrative made sense and fitted in with the witnesses' stories.

Perry clearly had an acute sense of his audience's tastes. The anecdotes he told with most relish were clearly designed to humiliate the Pinkertons. He claimed, laughing, that he had been under their noses all the time, and had even been out walking with agents who were holding the flyer with his photograph. Perry knew that many of the public would be on his side. The agents' work as strike breakers made them targets of radical condemnation but they were also despised by country people for their city arrogance and by others for their underhand tactics. When agents hurled a bomb into Jesse James's home, killing his young stepbrother and blowing off his mother's arm, their attack on the family affronted public decency and won sympathy for the outlaw. Perry made his own feelings clear: 'I hate Pinkerton men. I have nothing but contempt for them. They are nothing but the scum of cities, though I wish to except from this assertion some of the officers. I was working on the Fitchburg Railroad when, during the strike on the New York Central, Pinkerton men were employed, and though I probably only disliked them before I hate them since.' Local reporters were glad of a chance to mock the Pinkerton detectives for their failure to catch a man who had 'finally been landed by rural officers in a rural jail'.

Justice, meanwhile, moved swiftly. The first stage of Perry's arraignment took place the day after his arrest. In the afternoon of Monday, 23 February he was charged with two offences – shooting at an engine and assault in the second degree on the engineer of the freight train whose engine he stole. The main purpose was to enable the Wayne County lawmen to hold Perry until Daniel McInerney had recovered sufficiently to testify. Then Perry could be charged with breaking into an express car and assault with intent to kill.

The first hearing took place before Justice Theodore Fries and years later his grandson Theodore Harry Fries, nine years old at the time, recalled the scene. Word spread that Perry was being brought out, and as he was marched through the streets, handcuffed to Deputy Collins, people filled the sidewalks and leaned out of windows to catch a glimpse of him. Some even clambered on to rooftops to get a better view.

Amateur photography was the newest fad at the time and the local dentist set up his camera in the street, hoping to catch the desperado as he passed. In an age of slower shutter speeds, when newspapers still employed artists to illustrate their reports, it seems unlikely that this early paparazzo would have been successful. In any case Perry, much to the frustration of the crowd, had covered his face with a white handkerchief. Sharp observers noted that it was silk. The effect was tantalizing. All the crowd could see of the infamous Perry was his eyes.

Justice Fries's office was not large, so nearly all the furniture had to be removed to make room for the participants and spectators. Sheriff Thornton's party and the lawyers were forced to squeeze past dozens of people standing on the stairway leading to the office. Perry looked slightly pale and both he and Collins lost their hats in the scramble, but, as one reporter observed, he was 'perfectly collected, his piercing eyes staring boldly into the faces which surged around him'.

Young Theodore Harry took refuge from the sea of legs, standing on top of a desk that was also a convenient vantage-point. In the rush and crush, coats were torn, hats trampled, and pictures on the wall broken. The room was so tightly packed that when Theodore Harry's grandfather felt faint in the middle of the hearing, he had to be passed over the heads of the crowd to the door. It was some time, his grandson recalled, before the elderly gentleman saw the funny side of his undignified exit.

Perry's response to being charged was both assured and surprising. 'I have no counsel and I want none,' answered Perry. 'I will argue my own case. I plead not guilty.' He had gained some control in jail by making a confession but that no longer suited his purpose. He kept up his new image of the witty performer, amusing the court by playing word-games and chopping logic with the witnesses just like a real lawyer. But he had a serious intention: pleading not guilty gave him a chance to try to undermine the charge of shooting with intent to kill, the most serious he faced. In his cross-examination, he asked the witnesses if they could swear that the shots he fired at the engine were aimed to kill. Both men admitted that they could not. Justice Fries decreed that there was, nevertheless, a case to be heard by the next Grand Jury.

If Perry was disappointed he made no sign but when he was escorted to the police court to face the next charge, the crowd began to annoy him and he muttered, 'I'll hire a hall and give an exhibition of myself. The people act like a lot of cattle or bronchos on a ranch out west.' There were clearly limits to the performer's patience.

Perry soon regained his composure and scored a few points cross-examining witnesses in the second hearing but was again held for Grand Jury trial on $3,000 bail. It was judged highly unlikely that anyone would stand such a high bail, but if someone did, the Lyons authorities were prepared. They announced that they would simply charge Perry on another count and take him back into custody. Perry would be in the Butternut Street jail for a long time: the regular Grand Jury hearing was many weeks away.

Standing quietly at the back of the courtroom while the witnesses were examined was a respectable-looking middle-aged man. He was Oliver H. Perry, the accused's father. As the hearing ended Perry walked up and kissed him, reassuring him that everything would be all right. Back in the jail, the two men talked through the grilled corridor door and the father asked if he could give Perry some oranges, his favourite fruit. It was a rare moment of intimacy for the man who had been performing for days.

When his father was searched, as a matter of routine on leaving the jail, nobody expected to find anything. But in the respectable builder's pocket was a pencil drawing of a key with a message in Perry's handwriting: 'make of very hard wood, be sure and not get it brittle, for it must be very tough and strong make it about the size of this drawing. Hole in key 3/8 of inch. make the key blade so thick as it is drawn above.' It was a guide to making a key to the corridor door.

The discovery of an escape plan was a real embarrassment. Perry had clearly been plotting escape from the moment he arrived in the jail, while he was charming reporters and playing the lawyer, and the Lyons men had suspected nothing. Pinkerton *make of very hard Wook be sure and not get it brittle, for it must be very tough and strong make it about the tho size of this drawing Hole in key 3/8 of inch make the key blade so thick as it is drawn above*

FAC-SIMILE OF THE NOTE PERRY WROTE TO HIS FATHER.

Perry's drawing.

detectives were still hanging around the jail, looking for evidence that the Lyons lawmen were incompetent. Now they seemed to have found it. Thornton reacted swiftly, calling in a local blacksmith who riveted heavy iron shackles linked by an eight-inch-long log chain round Perry's ankles.

Cool as he seemed on the surface, Perry was clearly determined to be free. Asked why he had tried to escape, he replied quite simply, 'Did you ever know a bird to be imprisoned and did not try to get free?' And when his plan was frustrated he took the chance to make fun of his keepers, commenting wryly, 'I think you ought to get a jail strong enough to hold me without this. I ain't very hard to hold.' Was this reaction, like his mockery of the detectives hunting him after the first robbery, just youthful bravado, or a symptom of the same reckless streak that had led to his arrest? It certainly made the lawmen even more determined to avoid further embarrassment. He went on to joke that shackles were often called 'Irish Charms'. But the officers noticed that when he walked these charms were slippery, as his feet, which were long and slim, looked as though they could slip through the shackles. They swiftly ordered the blacksmith to fit a new, tighter pair. Again Perry reacted with some swagger: 'I think these people must be afraid of me for they anchor me down as if I was a giant.'

46

Perry's escape attempt revealed his ability to conceal his real purposes. It also pointed to a complicated family history. Oliver H. Perry had vehemently insisted that he had no idea that the drawing had been slipped into his pocket. The lawmen had no proof that he was lying but some reason to doubt him. He seemed respectable enough, living and running his building business in a decent road in Syracuse, but he had had his own run-ins with the police, usually over scams to pay off debts. Eventually they released him without charge, but banned him from visiting his son again. Thornton and Collins pretended to Perry that his father had betrayed him and he seemed to believe them, complaining loudly about not being able to trust anyone. They were obviously trying to undermine his confidence, but was he just feigning anger and hurt to keep his father out of more trouble? Or was there, as some observers thought, a hint of real doubt and anxiety in his reaction? The lies both men told about their relationship made it hard to know.

When his father had first been questioned about Perry, he claimed not to have seen him for many years, after an earlier estrangement, but he was clearly lying. Neighbours testified that a man identical to Perry, going under the name of Mr Hopkins, had visited Oliver H. and his wife Sarah just before the recent robbery. They remembered him particularly because he had shown off a strange object: a pickled human ear. Perry adamantly denied visiting his family and, despite his scheme with the drawing of the key, and his show of anger at his supposed betrayal, seemed determined to protect his father from involvement in his current predicament. With his father banned from the jail, Oliver Perry kept in contact by writing, while his father began to give his own interviews to the press about the son from whom he had supposedly been estranged. Mrs Perry, a striking woman, visited the jail with clean clothes but did not stop to see her son. Her behaviour seemed as odd as her husband's was slippery. What mother, knowing her son was shackled in a cell, would not seek to comfort him?

Clean clothes would clearly have been welcome, even if they did not come with comfort, as the contents of Perry's valise revealed that he had a definite liking for the finer things in life. As well as the drawing of the key, Perry had given his father a ticket to reclaim a valise from storage. Detectives followed him back to Syracuse, impounded the case and took it back to Lyons for examination. Its contents were fascinating, offering proof of some of the known facts of Perry's past and tantalizing hints of others yet to be revealed.

An expensively bound Bible with many passages underlined and marked in red ink appeared to indicate that Perry had indeed shown religious inclinations, as the citizens of Troy had insisted after his first robbery. One underscored passage read: 'For the weapons of our warfare are not carnal but mighty through God even to the pulling down of strongholds' (Corinthians X: 11). The Bible also showed Perry's determination to conceal his identity. It had clearly been a gift and bore his name imprinted in gold letters on the cover. A date remained, 1891, but the name had been scratched out with a knife.

More religious cards and pamphlets were bundled together in a leather case, along with a red railroad flag and a long-blade butcher's knife, its blade spattered to the hilt with what one paper luridly called spots of 'blood rust', cartridges and tools for cleaning revolvers. Other items included the smoked-glass spectacles Perry wore as a disguise, some fine silk underwear, a pillbox with the place of purchase scratched off, a mouth organ, a buckskin bag containing Mexican coins and two pieces of gold wire, probably from broken jewellery, a Spanish–English phrase book, published in Mexico City, an 'indecent book in Spanish', that sat rather oddly with the religious reading matter, and a glass jar containing the severed ear of a black man.

The ear was final proof that the son had been visiting his family just before the robbery, but, although they were sheltering him, there was no evidence that they had been aware of his plans to rob the second train. The ear gave Perry a chance to display his rather dark sense of humour, as he teased reporters that he had killed the ear's original owner and had planned to send it to the detectives. He eventually revealed that it was a souvenir of a night-time visit to a dissecting room with some medical students he had lodged with while on the run.

The most intriguing find was a small collection of photo-graphs, all of women. Two were in an expensive, Russian leather pocketbook. The third was in a frame. The photographs in the pocketbook were in sharp contrast to each other. One, a cabinet photograph taken in Wilmington, Delaware, was of what the papers called 'a coarse-faced woman'. The other, a tintype, showed a girl in her early teens. Entwined about it was a braid of jet-black hair. The framed photograph was of a plain-looking woman wearing spectacles. At the bottom of the picture, in Perry's handwriting, was the inscription, 'My Mother, December 21, 1891'. The woman in the photograph looked nothing like the Mrs Perry who had been seen in Lyons. Who were these women in Perry's life and where were they now as he sat shackled in his cell awaiting his trial?

If the mystery women had so far failed to appear, plenty of

others had flocked to Butternut Street to see the famous outlaw. Perry's reactions to being expected to 'perform' ranged from angry resistance to charm. When men were allowed into the cellblock to see him, he often turned his face to the wall or covered his face, telling Sheriff Thornton that for all he knew they might be Pinkerton detectives. He was much happier to see the dozens of female visitors, both young and old, many of whom brought gifts of books, flowers, fruit, candies and other treats. Among them was Mrs Goetzman who had apparently forgiven him for taking her favourite mare. While plenty of men expressed a grudging admiration for his daring, something made women in particular take to the young robber. Perhaps it was his looks and daredevilry, or the boyish charm that seemed to enrage the detectives. Whatever the attraction, here was a young man in trouble, a captive prodigal son who seemed to have no lover or mother ready to comfort him.

Not everyone approved. The Reverend Dr Ostrander, a local Presbyterian minister, roundly condemned the women of Lyons in his sermon for their wicked folly in gratifying the vanity of a criminal, and some reporters took their chance to reprimand the fairer sex whose appetite for news of Perry they kept feeding. One paper censoriously announced: 'Flowers for Perry: Woman's Mawkish Sentimentalism Again Manifests Itself', yet kept featuring Perry stories almost daily. 'The law,' Perry observed after the Reverend Ostrander's sermon, 'rigid as it is, is a great deal more charitable than some people's Christianity.'

Disapproving clerics and hypocritical reporters did little to stem public enthusiasm for Perry. While their parents could visit the jail, the local children busied themselves taking turns to play the robber or the lawman in noisy re-enactments. Or, as Theodore Harry Fries remembered, they crowded the sidewalk outside Ed Walter's second-hand store. There, in the window, was a large crayon drawing of the scene of Perry's capture, showing the robber at bay behind the brick wall, brandishing his guns. To the nine-year-old and his friends, the picture was as good as the movies would be to their own children, and Perry was a real-life hero and villain rolled into one.

CHAPTER 5

'I lived a wild life . . .'

I N T H E weeks when everyone waited for the trial that would decide Oliver Perry's future the young robber started to reveal more about his past. In his cell in Lyons, smoking cigars provided by grateful reporters, he began spinning together fantasy and reality in stories that would enthral an eager public who wanted to know everything about Oliver Perry.

Shortly after Perry's arrest, his father had claimed that he and his son were related to Oliver Hazard Perry, naval hero of the War of Independence, and to August Belmont, the influential New York financier. For many, this was final confirmation that Oliver Curtis Perry was no ordinary thief. He already had good looks, intelligence, daring and a kind heart, if the rumours of gifts to the needy were to be believed. Now he had an illustrious lineage. But while his father was certainly named after Commodore Perry, the kinship, if any, was distant. Yet if Perry's lineage was not as illustrious as his father asserted, his life, according to his own stories, was as dramatic as his crimes.

Few of these 'revelations', some of which were undoubtedly inventions, can be verified now, without reliable records to distinguish fact from fiction. But they fascinated press and public alike, building a mythology around Perry that tapped into the fantasies of his age: of a Wild West that was swiftly being tamed, of Mexico, a land of passionate rebels and sensual delights, and of the fateful act that propelled an ordinary working man out of his unrewarding daily grind into the world of wealth. Perry evidently shared, and lived, some of these dreams. But he also knew their power.

Amidst the exaggerations and the fantasies were the bare bones of the story of a short but dramatic life. Perry described a boy from upstate New York who ran away to start a new life out west, as a ranch hand and cowboy. He said almost nothing about his childhood and gave few details of his western days, saying simply, 'It was a wild life and entering heartily into it I became wild and reckless.' Years later he would describe turning to crime with a gang of 'mates' in Texas and Nebraska, and hint that he had learned to rob trains in the west. But in 1892 he would only say that two or three years earlier he had tired of his wild life and decided to 'reform'.

In the hope of living a respectable life he returned to New York. There the wanderer settled in the city of Troy. One day he was encouraged by acquaintances to attend a prayer meeting at the Helping Hand mission, run by Miss Amelia Haswell, the woman who infuriated detectives by destroying Perry's photographs when he was on the run.

Amelia Haswell.

54

Amelia Haswell took a shine to him and he gradually trusted her enough to tell her about his troubled past and even began to call her 'Mother', the name inscribed on the photograph of her he carried in his valise. Convinced that he deserved a second chance, she helped him to get a job with a local railroad company, the Fitchburg, and even let him stay with her while he looked for lodgings. Perry started work as a brakeman, a dangerous job that involved running along the tops of cars on moving trains in order to reach the brakes between them. Later this skill would be a key to his daring robberies. But his church friends in Troy saw no signs of his future fall from grace. He made no secret of his 'sinful' youth, they said, but seemed to be genuinely trying to reform: he did not drink, would not tolerate swearing, joined the Railroad Young Men's Christian Association, and even asked to be excused from work on Sundays in order to attend services. He also showed early signs of his ability as a charismatic speaker to entertain and persuade an audience. Then he had been in demand at mission meetings, exhorting sinners to repent, while later he would charm the hardened men of the New York press and through them a growing band of supporters.

The Trojans were not the only ones to be convinced of Perry's sincerity. The Fitchburg line ran between Troy and North Adams in Massachusetts, through the newly built Hoosick tunnel. As a railroad worker, Perry lodged at both ends of the line and made a similar impression in both places. His North Adams landlady, Mrs Sutton, told the press that Perry was no trouble, and that another lodger, a young lady, had often played the organ and sung for him. He had given no hint of his criminal past, but his musical tastes might have offered a clue. His reading matter, Mrs Sutton recalled, was invariably devout, including a book, inscribed as a gift from Amelia Haswell, called *Precious Hymns for Times of Refreshing and Revival*. But his favourite song had been 'Seven Long Years I've Been in Prison'.

After about a year as a brakeman, Perry was seriously injured in an accident on the railroad. He was running along the top of a train when it entered the Hoosick tunnel and he was knocked on to the tracks, seriously injuring his back and fracturing his skull. When he was eventually discharged after a long stay in hospital, he was penniless and unemployed. Few jobs were held for injured employees and he received no sick pay. His church friends used their influence once again to find him a job, this time a less hazardous position on the New York Central passenger service between Albany and Syracuse, working inside the trains rather than on top of them. This meant a move to Albany, the state capital, where he worked until early May 1891 when he was given ten days' leave of absence for medical reasons. But at the end of that time, instead of returning to work, he handed in his notice and disappeared for some months. He never explained how or where he spent the summer months, but in mid-September he started work on the Central once more. Two weeks later he robbed the American Express Special.

Perry's explanations of his motivation in committing his first train robbery are an intriguing mixture of fact and fabulation. The immediate catalyst, he said, was a run-in with his trainmaster who had reprimanded him for a minor infringement of the company's uniform regulations. While being told off, he had, he said, experienced 'a feeling of rebellion which I was unable to overcome'. Clearly, being forced to conform and being rebuked by someone in authority had triggered more than normal levels of resentment. The young man who had lived a wild life out west was feeling increasingly trapped and exploited in the regulated world of the industrial east.

For a while he brooded on his situation, then saw a way of escaping it. 'As I stood there thinking I saw the express boxes being loaded upon the train and I thought of the wealth in those safes in the express car. I knew that my position meant drudgery and hard work for small pay all my life. I resolved to do something desperate, and naturally the safes in the express car were the first objects of my ambition.'

His resentment about his apparent lot in life may have been fuelled by a new influence. Amelia Haswell, who insisted on the sincerity of Perry's attempt to live a good Christian life up to that point, believed that he had been led astray in Albany by someone she called an 'Ingersoll man'. Robert Ingersoll was a free thinker whose radical views of subjects from equality to prison reform and atheism were popular with those campaigning against social and economic exploitation. As Perry's hostility towards the Pinkertons who had broken the Fitchburg strike had revealed, he held some views that might have been seen as radical. He told one reporter, 'When going through the country I used to compare my condition with that of the rich. . . . Remember, I didn't plunder from those who couldn't afford to be despoiled. Look on these hands. They are hard with honest toil and I would wear them to the bones at work before I would inflict a loss on anyone unable to sustain it. But I thought the American Express Company could sustain a little plucking and I set about it.'

Perry certainly resented being exploited but he was also quite capable of using the rhetoric of oppression to win public sympathy, and his claim not to have robbed the poor was at best naïve. It is, as ever in his interviews, hard to distinguish between truth and invention. Later he hinted that there had been another, far more personal, catalyst for his first train robbery.

'I wanted to settle down. I wanted to make a home. Of course, I had a reason for wanting to make that home. I wanted it to be as good as the homes I saw. I thought a great deal about it. I'd knocked about the world a good bit. I'd been earning my own living since I was eleven years old. I had never had a home of my own. I had never married, and I did not mean to marry until I thought I could make such a home as I'd thought about. I believed – I had reason to believe – that I should have the companion I wanted. I intended to go West and settle down and have a home. I intended to live a straight life and be an honest man. I'd been a wild boy, but I had come to the time when I was a man, when I would look my life over and think what I was going to make of it.' Realizing, he said, that an ordinary job would never pay enough, 'I thought this all over, and I saw the only way was a bold stroke, with big chances.' Tellingly, given his positively dangerous level of confidence, he added, 'I believed I was clever enough not to be found out.'

Perry only hinted at a romantic twist in his tale, and was always guarded in his references to it, but Amelia Haswell made it explicit. Towards the end of his time in the west, she said, he had worked for a time on a ranch in New Mexico where he had fallen in love with his employer's daughter and she with him. The young couple had gone riding together in his free hours and met in secret until her father found out, dismissed Perry and sent her away. Perry had resolved to prove he could be respectable and buy a decent home for them both. So he had moved back to New York, hoping to return for her when he had made enough money. According to Amelia Haswell, he 'could never speak of the girl without becoming nervous, and the tears would come into his eyes'.

But everything went wrong. Perry had already become disillusioned with the slow, small rewards of honest work when, sometime before the fall of 1891, he discovered that his 'sweetheart' was gravely ill and possibly dying. This, his friend assumed, was the reason for his leaving Albany in the summer months. In the early fall, Amelia Haswell received a letter from Perry that claimed he was enduring 'the greatest sorrow of my life' and was 'tempted almost beyond endurance'. She had been away on vacation when the letter arrived and by the time she had a chance to reply, her good counsel came too late. It was Perry's desperation to help his girl, Amelia Haswell believed, that made him take the greatest risk of his life and rob the express. Already convinced that he would never earn enough money honestly to match the gilded palaces of New York's robber barons, he now feared he would never be able to provide a modest home for his sweetheart. So he turned his railroading skills to his own, criminal, advantage. Then, evading capture in Utica, he made his way west, only to find that he was too late. His sweetheart had already died.

Perry told his own story of what happened next. 'I had the greatest disappointment a man can have. . . . So I never made that home and I never settled down. I was reckless then. The money was no good to me. I lived a wild life and I gambled the most of it away. I did not care what became of me, that is the truth.' A passing remark, possibly designed to test his audience's credulity, and certainly mischievous, led to a totally untrue story that Perry had tried to join up with the famous Mexican revolutionary Catarino Garza, struggling to overthrow the tyrannical President.

He certainly spent time in the border country where Garza fought, and then in Mexico, a country he loved: 'it is beautiful there – always summer . . . Everyone went promenading in the evening and there were bands of music and something going on all the time.' But Perry denied any involvement with Garza and talked instead about losing himself in his reckless life after the robbery and his sweetheart's death.

He insisted that he had never been a drinker, but admitted to having taken opium. His main diversion and vice, predictably in the light of his crimes, was gambling. Then, as Christmas approached, he decided to return to Troy. He was taking quite a risk, going back to one of the places where he was well known and where his friends were still being watched by the police and detectives. But it seems that Perry was tired of drifting, even in fine clothes, and wanted to see his 'Mother'.

On 22 December 1891 he turned up at Amelia Haswell's house and confessed the truth about his involvement in the robbery to her. She tried to persuade him to hand himself in, but he was afraid that his past record and the determination of American Express and the Pinkertons to make an example of him would guarantee a lengthy sentence in prison. He was particularly worried that he would end up in Clinton, the daunting institution in the far north-east of the state, known as 'Little Siberia'. In the end, he gave Amelia the jewellery to return to American Express, which she did, through a lawyer friend, and moved on.

If Amelia Haswell knew where he had gone, she said nothing. Her loyalty to Perry was extraordinary. She had not only destroyed her photographs of him when he was a wanted man, but had even called at the photographer's to ask that the glass negative be destroyed. In response, the detectives had her mail intercepted and kept her under almost constant surveillance from the first robbery and even while Perry was awaiting trial.

Perry spent the next two months in Canada, where he posted the letter exonerating Messenger Moore, and, sometime before the end of February, went to stay in Syracuse where he visited his family. There he decided on the biggest gamble of his life: robbing the American Express Special a second time. While he tried to explain the motivation for the first robbery at some length, Perry admitted that he committed the second on 'impulse', and to make money because 'I had lived a life that brought expensive tastes and unfitted me to go back to earning $2 a day.' As a wanted man, he must have had a stark choice: turn himself in and face a long prison sentence or live as an outlaw indefinitely. He clearly dreaded prison, so surrender was unthinkable. To live on the run cost money, to live even half-decently cost a great deal. Another robbery was the only solution, and why not try to repeat a success?

Perry's stories of his life up to the recent robbery made sensational reading in 1892 and throughout his life. Some parts were undoubtedly exaggerated, others made up. Over a century later it is not easy to establish the whole truth. Neither he nor Amelia Haswell ever named his doomed sweetheart and there is no documentary proof that she ever existed. But what respectable family would acknowledge that their daughter had planned to elope with a ranch hand, let alone one who became a notorious robber? The Pinkertons reported that Perry, as a man with a criminal record known to the eager agents, had been followed from Deming, New Mexico to Flagstaff and Tucson in Arizona in the summer of 1891, before the first robbery, and was seen in El Paso, Texas on 28 November, shortly afterwards. Was he just meeting up with old mates from his wilder days or was he travelling to find his sweetheart? There was one tangible clue to support the story: the photograph of the young girl, with the lock of dark hair wound around it, in Perry's wallet. Amelia Haswell said that both belonged to his sweetheart and had been carried by Perry since their meeting. She may have been naïve and the story certainly sounds like a romantic cliché designed to win sympathy, but it is possible to be too cynical. Some romances are true.

The stories of Perry's crimes, his tragic romance and shattered dreams made him an ever more appealing figure. Men and boys could imagine his wild cowboy days, as industrialization made the frontier seem more like a myth every day. Radicals and reformers could identify with the working man who had finally snapped under the weight of social and economic injustice. Romantics could feel for the sensitive but proud man, torn between right and wrong as he fought to build a life with the woman he loved. The man shackled in the Lyons cell was, if anything, even more alluring now than he had been as a handsome fugitive.

There were, of course, exceptions to the general enthusiasm, such as an anonymous letter sent to praise Deputy Collins and denounce Perry: 'I say most emphatically that if the Ladies will go to see this inhuman *Toad*, let them carry the *Cross Bones* and exhibit them, and for Dessert, paris green puddings, with strychnine flavoring, and to save the great vigilance of Watchmen, spike both feet solid to the floor, strip him naked, pack him in solid ice, smash of the hand he shot McInnery [*sic*] with, give him chop sticks in the other hand to eat with, shut out all light from his cell, and to add to the darkness shut the Nigger in with him, with a double barrelled shot gun, in this way you may rid yourselves of both.'

There was plenty of ammunition for less unhinged assaults on Perry's self-defined character, although the 'evidence' was as unreliable as that for his deeds of heroism and romance. Labourers' daughters and fine ladies alike claimed to have been engaged or even married to Perry, then deserted. He was accused of swindling businesses in Philadelphia, duping clergymen in Canada, robbing a traveller in California and, most seriously, of killing a Montana saloon keeper in a brawl. Perry roundly protested his innocence of all the charges and even found unexpected support from Pinkerton agents whose alleged sightings of the wanted man became useful alibis. He was never charged with any of the supposed crimes and such was the public interest in and support for him that the rumours simply added to his allure. A reporter conducted an opinion poll of local citizens and found that all but one would like to see Perry freed.

The Perry myth also had obvious commercial potential. In a bizarre realization of Perry's joke about making an 'exhibition' of himself, Robinson's Musee-Theater in Rochester boasted a new display: two figures of Oliver Curtis Perry in wax. One showed Perry in his famous train-robbing outfit, with hood and rope; the other depicted him 'as he would appear on the street'. Newspaper advertisements described the Musee-Theater's attractions:

In the curio hall the original Kawakamis, sword fencers and athletes from Japan, will be seen, their acts combining the three elements of curio, novelty and speciality. Mr. and Mrs. Kawakami will appear in the costumes of ancient Japanese

DESPERADO PERRY'S OUTLAW REGALIA.

Perry's train-robbing disguise as worn by Robinson's waxwork.

warfare. Miss Kate Koon, lightning artist, is announced to 'paint beautiful designs in two minutes'. The Hungarian gypsy band is there and there will be seen in wax a representation of Oliver C. Perry the daring train robber recently captured near Lyons.

Despite the exotic charms of these fellow attractions, it was the wax Perry that topped the bill. General admission to the Musee-Theater was 10 cents, with seats for shows from 15 cents and boxes at 25 cents. Doors were open from 1 p.m. to 10 o'clock at night.

When news of the exhibit reached Perry, he was not flattered. He hired a lawyer, through his Trojan friends, to demand that Robinson withdraw the exhibit or face an injunction. Displaying an extraordinarily canny sense of his value as a commodity, Perry calculated the price of his reputation as $10,000, the amount for which he threatened to sue Robinson. Robinson bullishly announced that new Perry figures would soon be exhibited in his Buffalo museum. However, in the next week's advertisement in Rochester, there was no sign of the Perry exhibit. The new star attraction was 'Prof. Dick's EDUCATED FLEAS. Flea Circus, Flea Actors, Flea Tricks'. Supporting the fleas, possibly in more ways than one, was Angola, 'the Only Living Gorilla in America'.

Perry's self-marketing was even more explicitly revealed in a letter he wrote to his father. He told him that he wanted him to have his possessions after his trial: 'I think you could take my clothes, satchel, revolvers, mask, hooks and rope, in fact all my things and sell them to some museum for a good round sum of money. I also will have some things sent to you in time that will make quite a collection. I have a large western hat cost $15.00, boots $12.00, two blankets, one saddle blanket and one bed blanket made by hand by the Indians, and a number of other things. I will have them sent to you just as soon as I think best. If you can consult some good lawyer and have him correspond with different Museum Managers and in that way perhaps you could get a good offer for the collection. I would not take less than $200.00 for the collection and I think you can get more.' The man who had risked everything in one last gamble may have lost but he was evidently determined to get some profit.

CHAPTER 6

'It's a long time to wait and
I don't like the idea'

WHILE HE was working the press, performing to the gallery and protecting his interests, Perry had also been busy behind the scenes. Since his foiled escape attempt soon after his arrest, he had seemed more concerned with charming the public at large than rejoining them. But in fact he had been plotting escape all the time and when his efforts were discovered a different side of his personality came to light.

First, the Sheriff disturbed Perry as he was trying out a half-finished lead key in the corridor door, resembling the wooden one he had sketched. The key was confiscated and the jail was searched. At first, the lawmen assumed Perry was being helped by an outsider, but soon they discovered it was an 'inside job' when they found more escape 'tools' hidden in other cells: lead foil that could have been melted over a lamp to form the key, pieces of wire to use to turn it, a steel strip, taken from the sole of a boot and sharpened, and a small piece of paper on which was scrawled 'We want it right off'. Evidently Perry and some of his fellow prisoners had been in league and the construction of a key for the corridor door had been merely the first stage in a plan. All the men were questioned and their answers kept secret.

Perry, whose own cell held no suspicious items, watched the entire search impassively. But one by one his plans to secure his freedom began to unravel. More tools were discovered hidden in an enlarged rat hole and eventually even Perry's clothing came under suspicion. First, the sacking wrapped round his shackles to stop them rattling was removed and the leg irons fell to the floor. He had cut them in two, using a small saw concealed in his Bible, which the Sheriff had let him keep for spiritual comfort. Amelia Haswell's gift had evidently been customized in a manner of which the missionary can hardly have approved.

If the Sheriff had been more thoughtful than careful when he first took Perry into custody, he was now determined to see, quite literally, that he had no more tricks up his sleeve. Perry was ordered to strip. All his clothes, the same ones he had worn when he was arrested and had, to his evident discomfort, been wearing ever since, were carefully examined. Then the lining of his jacket was ripped open. Sewn into the collar and waistband was a total of $250 dollars in $50 dollar bills. He had hidden them after the Utica robbery in case of emergency. Perry seemed so prepared and so determined to escape that, according to a report, nobody in Lyons believed 'he will come to trial without at least one fierce dash for liberty'. But his options were fast running out.

The Sheriff had to resort to stiff measures to contain his apparently incorrigible prisoner. Perry was moved to a smaller cell, only six by four feet, with a solid door rather than open bars, making it gloomy as well as cramped. He was told he was to be kept in close confinement until the trial and would have no unsupervised contact with other prisoners or visitors. Instead of eating in the corridor with the other prisoners, he would be fed in his cell. His meals would be passed through the small hole in

Wayne County Jail cellblock (From the collection of
the Wayne County Historical Society, Lyons, New York).

the upper part of the cell door. A watchman was to be stationed
outside his door, day and night.

Up until this point Perry had impressed people with his
apparent nonchalance, but the discovery of what was clearly a
careful plot and of the money that he might use for bribes or to
get equipment began to depress him. The man who enjoyed
telling tales clearly depended on his real plans being kept hidden.
Being in jail had not been that depressing, while he had the ability
to work on his fellow prisoners as carefully as he charmed the
press, to build a team around him and plan each stage of the
escape. Now he was back to square one. Close confinement
meant he had no chance of working on a new plan. He was
also beginning to suffer some pain as the result of an injury,

almost certainly a rupture, incurred during the long chase on horseback. Was the apparently indomitable Perry beginning to show signs of strain? He had also been warned that the Grand Jury hearing might not be until mid- June, two months away. 'It's a long time to wait and I don't like the idea,' he admitted but he was still defiant about the trial: 'I will plead not guilty. My sentence will be none the lighter if I do not.' He might be unable to escape what now looked like his certain fate, but clearly had no intention of taking his punishment meekly.

The discovery of one after another of his tools and activities also pointed to an inescapable conclusion that began to eat away at Perry. Someone had betrayed him. Isolated in his tiny cell and seeing his plans systematically frustrated, he turned his mind to the question of his betrayer's identity. He eventually decided it was a tramp known as 'One Armed Ed', who did chores in the jail. Ed suffered a twisted remaining arm as a punishment when he passed Perry his food, but was an innocent man. It was revealed much later that the informer had been another, younger prisoner who received a reduced sentence as a reward.

The growing strain on Perry showed when visitors tried to get a glimpse of the notorious prisoner, but even under pressure he managed to turn an unwelcome reality to some advantage. Although he was no longer allowed unsupervised visits from friends, local people and reporters still called at the jail and asked to see him. But when the officers allowed them to take a look through the cell door, Perry demonstrated a new technique for dealing with them. While the visitor tried, or asked, to see his face, he would turn towards a looking-glass in his cell. By watching them watching him he was exerting the only control he could as a prisoner, allowing people to see only what he wanted them to see.

Other visitors to his cell got harsher treatment as he began to take out his frustration on the jailers who had resorted to tough measures to contain him. Deputy Collins found him trying to break his shackles by dropping one of the legs of his iron bedstead on them. When guards tried to stop him he started hurling some heavy earthenware cups, which he had hoarded after meals, at them. As a punishment and to prevent similar incidents, his wrists were shackled, although when Collins tried to fit the new restraints he only avoided being covered with the contents of Perry's lavatory bucket by threatening the prisoner with his revolver. Perry's days of sitting with a cigar entertaining his visitors were definitely over. Until his trial he would be involved in regular skirmishes with his keepers, especially Deputy Collins.

Collins, made impatient by Perry's slipperiness and impudence, was reportedly keen to strip him of all his comforts, putting him on bread and water and even giving him a good thrashing if necessary. Sheriff Thornton, a milder man who was much more sympathetic towards his prisoner, had gone out of his way to treat him well, even writing to a newspaper to deny a report that Perry had obtained weapons to attack, and even kill, Collins. As the public awaited Perry's trial, the contrasting attitudes and approaches of the two lawmen became the subject of heated debate in their own right.

To some, Thornton was a gentle, kindly man who treated his young prisoner with sensitivity, to others, an indulgent fool who was being duped by a devious criminal, while Collins was seen as tough but fair, or, as Perry certainly believed, a licensed bully. It was a conventional enough debate

Deputy Sheriff
Jeremiah Collins.

about how to deal with criminals. But there was a particular twist to the story of Thornton versus Collins in the battle over Perry's treatment. Thornton was a Republican and stories about his apparent laxity versus the more effective approach of his Deputy appeared in the *Wayne Democratic Press*. The famous prisoner, who had used the press to win public support, had become a pawn in a game of local politics.

Sheriff Walter Thornton.

Inside the jail, Perry was more concerned with getting some personal revenge on Deputy Collins for his punitive approach. He wrote a jail diary, now lost, that included an account of his arrest in the swamp that was clearly designed to undermine Collins's claim to the reward for his capture. He claimed that he offered to surrender if Collins shared the $1,000 reward equally with him, or let him walk away unharmed and surrender instead to the crowd. When Collins agreed to share the reward, Perry let himself be captured, feigning the fight that had given rise to such praise for the Deputy's courage. But once Perry was in custody, Collins had conveniently forgotten the deal. While Perry may have hoped to damage the Deputy's reputation, and the diary was conveniently leaked to the press, nobody seemed to believe his version.

The long wait for the trial continued and, without new incidents, the press turned to other news. The harsh winter had turned to a milder spring, and May Day workers' marches, which many had believed would bring bloody revolution to Europe and provoke radical unrest nearer home, turned out to be peaceful protests. Of greater interest to readers looking for dramatic stories was the sad tale of George Hamilton, 'the screaming boy' of Kentucky. The fourteen-year-old, a bright chap with a 'genius in mechanical affairs', had been struck down by terrible headaches that left him deaf and blind and unable to taste the food that kept him alive. All he could do, his body so twisted by pain that his head was bent back to his hips, was scream. His doctors could do nothing, and on 7 May the screams finally stopped. Some torments were worse than any prison sentence.

CHAPTER 7

His Career Ended!

PERRY'S GRAND Jury hearing began, earlier than he had been led to expect, on 17 May. Predictably, the Wayne County Court House was filled to overflowing. Over the next two days more than forty witnesses were called (although one over-excited reporter gave a count of more than a hundred), including the entire crews of both trains Perry was alleged to have robbed, numerous detectives and members of the public. Before testifying, Burt Moore and Daniel McInerney, now apparently restored to health, called in at the jail to identify Perry as their attacker. Although McInerney insisted in court that the incident had not affected his mind, he was so anxious while in the jail that he hid behind Moore.

Almost as soon as the hearing started, a shocking drama unfolded that distracted press and public attention. One of the witnesses for the prosecution was a young New York City jeweller's store porter called Albert Stanton, who had been subpoenaed to appear to make a

Messenger Daniel McInerney.

formal identification of items stolen in the Utica robbery. The day after he testified, apparently without incident, he set off for home by train. Towards the end of the long journey, just after four in the afternoon, he suddenly stood up, walked into the middle of the carriage and said, 'Well, I might as well do it now.' Then he took out a pocket-knife and cut his throat from ear to ear.

He left a wife and three children and no clue to his brutal suicide. Stanton's life, up to this point, had been unremarkable. His employer suggested that anxiety about testifying in such a high-profile trial might have tipped him into insanity: 'I believe that he fairly worried himself into suicide.'

While such anxiety might have been enough to disturb someone who was mentally or emotionally fragile, it seems odd, if this was the reason, that Stanton did not kill himself on the way to the trial. The real reason for the suicide was never discovered. It may have been entirely unconnected to the trial. Whatever its catalyst, Albert Stanton's death was a sensational distraction from the hearing. It was also only the first of a series of tragedies to befall some of those whose lives became briefly entangled with Perry's.

Perry himself was formally arraigned on Thursday, 19 May. The large crowd, including a gallery full of women, was looking forward to a dramatic climax to Perry's time in Lyons and, indeed, his career. There had been much speculation about how he would plead, given his apparent determination after his long confinement to make a fight of it. A few days earlier he had been told that the District Attorney was subpoenaing his friend, Amelia Haswell, who had been bedridden by the strain of the detectives' constant pressure. The news that she would now have to make the long journey west strengthened Perry's resolve to force a trial and he engaged the services of a lawyer.

Just before he was called, the woman he called 'Mother' visited him in jail. The two spoke for a long time. Concerned about Perry's increasingly distressed and destructive behaviour, Amelia tried to persuade him that there was only one way to make the best of a hard situation, to take his punishment and trust in the Lord to protect him.

Perry was brought into court at five in the afternoon, heavily shackled and closely guarded. In a grey suit and with his moustache grown again, he looked as dashing as he had in his 'wanted' posters, but he was noticeably paler after months in jail. He spoke briefly with his attorney and was then asked to stand to hear the indictments against him.

The room was silent as the District Attorney read the indictments. The first was for burglary in the third degree, second offence, and robbery, first degree, second offence, both committed in Herkimer County on 30 September 1891. This indictment was for breaking into an express car and committing robbery by taking property in the care of Messenger Moore, to the amount of $5,000. The second was for burglary, first degree, second offence, assault, first degree, and attempt at robbery, first degree. This indictment was for breaking into the express car in Cayuga County, and attacking Messenger McInerney on 21 February 1892. The third was for assault in the first degree on Alexander McGilvery, the engineer of freight engine No. 511, whom Perry drove from his engine at gunpoint when trying to escape. The fourth and final indictment was for discharging firearms at a locomotive.

Most people expected Perry to put up a fight. But after each indictment was read, he spoke only one word: 'Guilty.' Amelia Haswell was convinced, and had convinced him, that this would encourage a merciful, lighter sentence. Perry may have taken her advice, but when he entered his plea his voice was almost inaudible. The realization that he was willingly committing himself to the incarceration he dreaded, and had fought so bitterly to avoid, must have been hard to bear. The District Attorney immediately asked that sentence be pronounced. The judge, William Rumsey, following the letter of the law, informed Perry that he was officially entitled to two days' respite before sentencing. The public strained to hear Perry's faltering reply: 'I have no reason as far as I am concerned.'

A *New York Herald* reporter commented that 'the whole scene was as businesslike and free from excitement as if the business before the Court were the argument of a technical motion involving a question of $10 costs'. But when Judge Rumsey pronounced his sentence it was clear that justice was not only swift but severe.

Perry was sentenced to five years for the first count of the first indictment, and twenty years on the second count, five years on the second indictment, ten years on the third indictment, and nine years and three months on the fourth indictment. The sentences were to be served as hard labour in Auburn prison and were to run, not as sentences often do today concurrently, but consecutively. In all he was to serve forty-nine years and three months. Even by the standards of the day, it was a harsh sentence.

'Half A Century Hard' was how one paper described it. If he survived, he would be released at the age of seventy-five in the almost unthinkable year of 1942. Perry listened to the sentence without any obvious show of emotion. One Lyons reporter interpreted his expression: 'Perry received his sentence as meekly as an erring child receives a mother's kind reproof. The bravado had left him. The wild western spirit had died away and the most noted desperado of the East, perhaps of the country, quailed before the verdict of grim justice.'

Swift calculations of the time Perry would serve, with reductions for 'good behaviour', were published, amounting to a term of twenty-nine years, four months and twenty-three days. In this case he would be released on 13 October 1921 at the age of fifty-six. But few who had witnessed, or read about, his escape attempts and refusal to knuckle down to life in jail believed his sentence would not be served in full. If he tried the same tricks in Auburn he would learn what the real penalties for insolence could be. A formality that followed his sentencing added a slightly chilling note to the hearing, as Perry's will was approved. In it he bequeathed his personal effects, including $300 cash and a diamond ring to his father, and his pistols to Sheriff Thornton.

Although he seemed to have been in a daze during the hearing, Perry swiftly rallied, laughing and talking as he returned to the jail, and set about preparing for the following day's move to Auburn. The prison's reputation was as fearsome as his was daring, but Oliver Perry was clearly determined to put on a show of defiance.

CHAPTER 8

Perry Dons the Stripes

THE PEOPLE of Lyons had one last chance to see Oliver Perry before he disappeared into prison. As he was taken to the station to catch the train to Auburn, he treated them to one last display of celebrity behaviour, giving mementos to a small group of people, including his lawyers and some newspaper correspondents. Each lucky man or woman was presented with a Mexican coin or piece of gold, a tiny share in Perry's exotic adventures and ill-gotten gains.

When they reached the station, the crowd was so big it was hard for the Sheriff and his men to get Perry through to the train. Once they were in the car, the crowd surged forward to surround it. Perry seemed tense and muttered about not being able to breathe. Twenty minutes passed before the train finally pulled out to make the journey east to Auburn.

The party soon had to change, at nearby Geneva, and this time some of the crowd managed to get inside the train. One man, apparently very drunk, lunged at Perry, shouting that he was going to give him a good thrashing. Sheriff Thornton moved swiftly to protect his prisoner. He had the man removed from the car, then locked the door to prevent further incidents as the train moved on. Perry relaxed a little and started reading a newspaper, commenting on the speculation about his possible release in 1921 for good behaviour: 'Boys, come over when I'm discharged and we'll all have an oyster supper.'

At the next stop, Waterloo, the crowd stayed on the platform, but a young lady who was leaving the train approached the party. Ignoring her mother's protests, she handed Perry a small bunch of lilies of the valley. He thanked her and placed the flowers in his buttonhole. But, although he was clearly still trying to maintain, or live up to, his romantic image, the constant attention, both aggressive and solicitous, was wearing him down. So at the next stop, when people asked to see the famous Perry, they were pointed not to him but to a guard in plain clothes. It was a simple ruse, but effective. After all, which man was handcuffed to which? It even fooled a newspaper correspondent who 'snapped' the wrong man and left contentedly to the cheers and laughter of the passengers 'in the know'.

The mood was still light as they continued to Aurelius. The conductor, making his rounds, asked Perry for his ticket. But after it had been punched earlier in the journey, Perry had given it to a bystander as a souvenir. So he jokingly suggested the conductor put him off the train. At Cayuga the train stopped for ten minutes for refreshments and Perry asked for some luncheon. Sheriff Thornton told him he would eat at Auburn but some other passengers went to buy him oranges. He ate two while plans were made for the imminent arrival in Auburn. As he saw the prison through the window, he was heard to mutter, 'I now have a home.'

The crowds hoping to see him enter his new home had been gathering since the early morning. Auburn had seen some desperate criminals but few as exciting as Perry. Men and women had rushed to the station to meet each New York Central train, hoping he would be aboard. Others waited outside the prison gate. By noon both places were teeming. Perry and his escorts finally arrived at the depot just before 1 o'clock. The crowd watched him climb down from the train, handcuffed to one guard, and escorted by another, then followed them out into the street. But the 'prisoner' they followed was really a young reporter from Lyons, and his 'guards' were other newsmen.

The real Perry and his party had waited for the decoys to draw the crowd, then walked undisturbed to the ironically named 'Home' restaurant, where a good dinner was ordered for everyone. Thornton meant to give Perry one last treat, but it was not a wise move. As word spread about his whereabouts, people rushed to stand outside the restaurant. When the time came to leave, the Sheriff had to call the police to clear a path through the crowd. Eventually they reached the imposing entrance to Auburn.

In its early days, reformers, government representatives and experts, including Alexis de Tocqueville and Gustave de Beaumont, travelled from across the world to visit Auburn. Built in 1816, it was the home of the 'Auburn system', a once-revolutionary penal regime at a time when the idea of reforming prisoners was still new. This involved convicts sleeping in individual cells, instead of shared rooms as they had hitherto, and working together in the day, but in total silence at all times. This double isolation was idealistically designed to encourage them to contemplate their own mistakes, without the corrupting influence of other criminals, and, pragmatically, to make them easier to manage by removing the possibility of plotting against the authorities. Although the men found ways of communicating,

Auburn Prison (Courtesy of Cayuga Museum).

a prisoner discovered talking at any time, unless responding to an officer's question, was subject to instant and severe punishment.

The Auburn regime was a modification of the even more extreme 'Pennsylvania system', which isolated prisoners in individual cells twenty-four hours a day, even for work. Auburn tried this in 1821, locking eighty prisoners in individual cells. The effects were dramatic. By the summer of 1823, it was found that total isolation had driven many of the men insane. When one cell door was opened, its occupant ran out and threw himself off the fourth-floor landing; another banged his head against the wall until he lost an eye. So Auburn decided to allow prisoners to work together, but in silence. Apart from being less obviously inhumane, this was also more economically practical. Prisoners locked in cells could only be employed in handicraft rather than more lucrative industrial production. In the nineteenth century prisons, with a slave labour force, had real economic potential.

By allowing 'congregate' labour, Auburn thrived. In 1892 it had a foundry as well as workshops producing goods from pearl buttons and furniture to brooms and boilers. It even, briefly, ran a silk factory. Commercial companies started to object to unfair competition from prison industries, and by 1895 New York's prisons would only be allowed to manufacture goods for their own use. But when Perry arrived, Auburn was, supposedly, an ideal blend of theory and practicality, a model society run according to the twin principles of industry and discipline.

Auburn created many of the features of prison life that swiftly became visual clichés, such as striped prison uniform and close-cropped hair to symbolize the convict's changed status. The prison also introduced a special walk, called 'lockstep', in which each prisoner shuffled along, holding the man in front, as they moved between cells and workshops or the dining hall. Lockstep, as the name suggests, turned men into a human chain. It also served as an abiding mark of their convict status. Years after they were released, when their hair had grown and uniform was a bad memory, ex-prisoners could be identified by the way they walked,

Prisoners in Lockstep (Courtesy of Cayuga Museum).

pushing their feet along as if still in lockstep. Auburn had recently shown its pioneering spirit yet again, and acquired a new notoriety, when, in 1890, William Kemmler became the first man in America to die in the electric chair.

Today Auburn's fearsome reputation has been eclipsed by the violent riots in neighbouring Attica, and its ivy-covered entrance makes the maximum-security prison look almost cosy. Yet inside the tension is still palpable. There may be a gym and a garden, as well as work and education, to occupy bodies and minds, but the men, mainly young African-Americans from downstate, are still obliged to walk in silence in the corridors so that the officers can be heard and no fights can be masked by inmates talking. Conversation in the yard is no longer forbidden, but the strangeness and strain of this male society are immediately apparent to a visitor. A woman walking through the yard on a hot summer's day, unseasonably dressed in trousers and a long-sleeved shirt, is palpably aware of the now hidden violence of these men's constraints. Nothing is said, but hundreds of staring eyes speak clearly.

Perry walked through the gate into Auburn just after 2 o'clock. Inside his new 'home', Mr and Mrs Perry were waiting. But before anyone could speak, the Warden intervened: 'Bring that man this way; he's my prisoner now.' He had not taken kindly to waiting while his prisoner had been dining at leisure. Perry tried to speak to his father but was hurried away. In the keepers' hall his handcuffs were removed and then he was swiftly marched to the barber's shop where he was stripped, dressed in prison uniform, his hair clipped short and his moustache shaved.

When he was next seen by those who had escorted him from Lyons, the change was shocking. He had arrived in a suit and hat with the bunch of lilies of the valley still in his buttonhole, quite the gentleman, if only in appearance. In a worn, stained uniform he seemed to have been stripped of more than his smart clothing. The process, called 'dressing in', was designed, as it is today, to transform the criminal into a prisoner, to strip and shear away individuality. It remains one of the most dramatic and symbolic acts that marks the attempted reduction of a man to an inmate.

Although the Warden was keen to process him as quickly as possible, Perry managed to do one last thing before he was taken away. He turned to the Sheriff who had treated him with kindness and made a small presentation. Perry was reduced to wearing 'the stripes' but when he left Auburn, Walter Thornton was newly adorned with Perry's gold collar stud and a pearl scarf pin. He returned home to face accusations of 'bad taste' in giving Perry a last good dinner, and a few months later died suddenly in his sleep of a suspected heart attack. Deputy Collins fared much better, later becoming his county's best-known sheriff, remembered until his death for capturing Perry.

It was assumed that in Auburn Perry would disappear from public view. Reporters would find it less easy to interview the apparently ever-willing speaker in prison than in the County Jail, and he would have no easy way of addressing the public through them. But the mythologizing of Oliver Perry continued all the same. Just a day after he was sentenced, *The NY Central Train Robbery, Or, the Nerviest Outlaw Alive*, was published. Priced at 5 cents, it was Number 42 in the 'Nick Carter Library', subtitled 'The Best 5 Cent Library of Detective Stories'. The series was one of the most popular collections of pocket-sized 'dime novels' that offered easily concealed adventure to youngsters and their parents. The latest edition told the story of fictional detective Nick Carter's involvement in the downfall of the very real train robber. Framed by an imagined conversation between Nick Carter and Jerry Collins, totally inaccurate fantasies of Perry's outlaw life as a crack shot and hardened killer as well as debonair deceiver were interwoven with facts to create a character to match his western counterparts, Billy the Kid and Jesse James. In popular fiction, as well as public opinion, Perry had joined the outlaw elite.

The real Perry was in trouble just days after his arrival. It was not, this time, because of his attitude, arguing with his keepers or trying to escape, but it would still have a dramatic impact on his mood and on his future. He had been sent immediately to work in the foundry, but the heavy labour had caused the rupture that had only given him discomfort in Lyons to make him seriously ill. Unable to work, the man who hated confinement was locked up in his cell all day, except for mealtimes. It gave him plenty of time to think, to plot and also to brood.

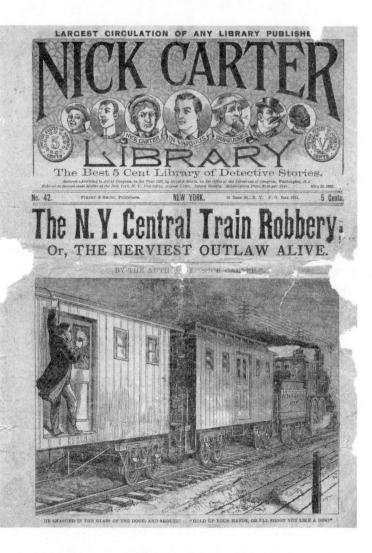

Nick Carter Library
(Courtesy of Onondaga Historical Association Museum
& Research Center, Syracuse, NY).

Just weeks later he was in real trouble after attacking a 'life man' called John Bender. The two men quarrelled at dinner and, to everyone's amazement, Perry produced two knives, threw one to Bender and challenged him to fight. When Principal Keeper James Shaw interfered, Perry surrendered. Whatever the ostensible reason for the fight, Perry had shown the other men what he was made of. Bender was an unpopular prisoner who regularly 'peached' on others, a good target for a new man who needed to show his mettle. All new prisoners have to prove themselves to avoid victimization. For a celebrity like Perry, as he was assessed by inmates and keepers, this was doubly important. His fame might easily make him a target for others. Also, as his time in Lyons had shown, he liked to win the support of those around him.

Perry paid a heavy price for his skirmish. His punishment, decided by Keeper Shaw, was nine nights in the dungeon. The dungeon cells were in the dimly lit basement, with bare stone walls and floors and no windows. When Perry was brought in, the first barred door would have clanged shut and then a second, solid oak door would have been locked, leaving him in total darkness. While he was effectively blinded, his other senses would, to make matters worse, have become more acute. The walls of the basement dungeons frequently ran with damp and crawled with vermin, although the bedbugs that plagued the normal cells would have been absent because there were no beds and no bedding. Prisoners sent to the dungeons were expected to sleep on the bare floor. They were also stripped of most of their clothing, supposedly to prevent suicide.

The cold would have been almost unbearable but any warmth would have intensified the stench rising from the uncovered bucket that served as a lavatory. And this dark, damp, cold and foul-smelling world was also silent. Regular cells in which prisoners were held in solitary confinement might allow precious whispered conversations when the guard was out of earshot, but in the dungeon the double doors sealed a man up as if he was in a tomb. The press frequently called any prison a 'living tomb', but the dungeon really merited the description. To the isolation that had driven men insane in the earlier experiment was added almost complete sensory deprivation. In the dungeon Perry would have been totally disoriented. The only way of telling day from night would have been when, once a day, the outer door opened and he would be given a piece of bread, weighing not more than two ounces. From a tin cup held by a guard he would have been able to drink two ounces of water. Then the door would shut and darkness would return for another twenty-four hours. Apart from occasional visits by a silent physician to check his pulse, this would be his only human contact.

Few prisoners' memories of the dungeon were recorded, but two accounts suggest its horrors. Alexander Berkman was a Russian-born anarchist, sentenced to twenty-two years in prison, shortly after Perry, for the attempted assassination of an industrialist. On his release, he recollected a spell in a dungeon in another prison that was nearly identical to the one Perry occupied in Auburn.

'Utterly forsaken! Cast into the stony bowels of the underground, the world of man receding, leaving no trace behind . . . Eagerly I strain my ear – only the ceaseless, fearful gnawing [of rats]. I clutch the bars in desperation – a hollow echo mocks the clanking iron. My hands tear violently at the door – "Ho, there! Any one here?" All is silent. Nameless terrors quiver in my mind, weaving nightmares of mortal dread and despair. Fear shapes convulsive thoughts: they rage in wild tempest, then calm, and again rush through time and space in a rapid succession of strangely familiar scenes, wakened in my slumbering consciousness.

'Exhausted and weary I droop against the wall. A slimy creeping on my face startles me in horror, and again I pace the cell. I feel cold and hungry. Am I forgotten? Three days must have passed, and more. Have they forgotten me?'

Berkman, a man of courage and intelligence, had been in the cell for only one day. The effects of a single night in the Auburn dungeon would form the climax to the reformer Thomas Mott Osborne's searing 1912 indictment, *Within Prison Walls*, based on time spent undercover as a prisoner. His description of how he felt when about to be released from the dungeon suggested the profound psychological damage such isolation could also cause: 'I find myself wondering why I am not ready to shout with joy, and I discover it is because I feel as if all power of emotion has been crushed out of me. It is not merely utter and hopeless fatigue; it is as if something had broken inside of me; as if I could never be joyous again . . .' Osborne's reaction was tempered by his knowledge that he would be released. The real victims of the dungeon, like Perry, would have had no such sense of control. A prisoner in the dungeon was stripped of all the simple features of human society; he was reduced to a blind, bare creature, sustained on a starvation diet, locked in a lonely world from which he might never escape.

In this world present fears or guilt about the past could be magnified to the point of inducing severe depression and even temporary psychosis. The nightmares and hallucinations of many prisoners would gradually become their reality. At the end of their punishment many appeared docile, but this was rarely contrition, whatever the authorities claimed. Exhausted and desperate men would say anything to get out, but even then the punishment was not over. Some prisoners were so disturbed they were declared insane, some attempted suicide or self-harm. Men from the dungeons were also condemned to seek out the shadows even when they were returned to the light. After days or weeks of gloom, even pale winter sunlight through a barred window could cause intense pain. For those trying to control unruly prisoners, the dungeon was also a double-edged weapon. It offered at best a deterrent and a temporary control; at its worst it turned the difficult into the truly dangerous. In the long hours and days of isolation, dislike and distrust of the system and its representatives often turned to implacable hatred.

The horrors of the dungeon were confirmed by the least liberal of commentators. At an 1892 meeting of the National Prison Association, it was condemned by those urging a return to corporal punishment. One physician declared that although public sentiment condemned the flogging and paddling (the beating of prisoners with a flat wooden or leather paddle) that had been the norm until outlawed by the state legislature, the dungeon, or dark cell, was far more damaging. Corporal punishment was widely viewed as 'a relic of the dark ages', he argued, but the dungeon was a 'refinement of torture': 'It is a system of punishment which strikes not only at the physical power, it is a mental and moral degradation. It is not the confinement which produces a seeming submission, but it is the starvation and you have only inflicted a punishment when you have deprived the body of its rightful supply and this cannot be done without injury.'

93

Perry appeared to have submitted when he was released after nine days, but the authorities took no chances. They placed him in a brick-built cell in the centre of a row in the basement and he was not returned to work. The men who occupied the cells either side of his spent each day in the prison workshops, but he was locked up alone, twenty-four hours a day. The cell had a wire grating in front of the bars to prevent anyone from slipping him a knife or other implement with which to attack or escape, and a keeper prevented communication when other prisoners filed past on their way to work or eat. The keepers themselves were under strict instruction not to speak with the prisoner. So the young man who thrived on conversation and story-telling was isolated yet again.

Whatever the adverse psychological effects of such continuing isolation and lack of stimulation might have been, the keepers were pleased with its results. Over the next few months they reported that Perry was quite docile, and there were suggestions that he might eventually be returned to hard labour. But once again, Perry deceived his keepers. The brutal regime of the dungeon had certainly had an impact on him, but it had not broken his spirit or his resolve. With nobody to talk to and nothing to distract him, he turned his mind to the one thing that he still wanted above everything else: freedom.

On 23 October Oliver Perry escaped. The day before, when a keeper delivered his supper just after 4 o'clock, he saw nothing unusual although he commented later that Perry seemed to be in good spirits. But when the prisoners returned from work an hour later, the man who occupied a neighbouring cell called out that there was a hole in the dividing wall. The keepers ran to inspect it and found a large hole in the twelve-inch-thick wall. Perry must have dug when the other men were at work and concealed the hole with a towel. To their surprise, the keepers saw Perry was in his cot, sleeping through the commotion. But when they shook him, they found that the sleeping convict was really a bundle of clothes. He had waited until the keeper left, after seeing the other prisoners off to work, then wriggled through the hole and walked out of the open door of the neighbouring cell into the corridor. During the day only one keeper patrolled the wing, so he had no trouble in evading him and getting out into the yard. There he could hide in an outhouse until darkness fell to cover his final escape over the perimeter wall. The alarm was sounded and hours went by while guards searched every inch of the prison but to no avail.

Some time later a keeper saw someone walking swiftly across the prison yard from the foundry towards the collar shop. He shouted to him to stop but the man started running. Assuming it was Perry, the keeper fired a shot from his Winchester over his head and brought him to a halt near the pearl button shop, where another keeper jumped out of the shadows and struck him on the head with a heavy night stick. The blow was so powerful that the night stick broke in two. Perry fell to the ground, unconscious and bleeding heavily, and was carried into the Keeper's Hall. His head wound was washed but not judged serious enough for dressing, and he was then sentenced to twenty-five nights in the dungeon, to begin immediately.

To the embarrassment of his keepers, the story was swiftly leaked to the press. How could a man kept under such close surveillance have managed to dupe them so thoroughly? It seemed to have been only his own haste that was Perry's undoing. If he had paused to conceal the hole in the neighbouring cell after climbing through it, his absence might not have been noticed until after lock-up time. Then the guards on the perimeter wall came off duty, and he would most likely have been able to scale it to freedom. The mistake was uncharacteristic of his usually careful planning – the rest of the preparations suggest that he was as meticulous as ever. He was almost certainly disturbed at the last minute.

His capture was as controversial as his escape was shocking. Although the keepers insisted they had warned Perry before knocking him down, anonymous sources claimed this was untrue. Although he had been judged fit for immediate punishment, all the reports stressed the severity of the blow that felled him and some claimed he might die. The most damning report was from an Englishman called Edgar Moulton who was visiting Auburn on behalf of the Prison Reform Society and claimed to have witnessed the capture: 'The assault on the prisoner seemed to me to be entirely uncalled for and unprovoked. I have visited the prisons of the czar. Much as they are to be condemned, I have never seen or heard of a single brutality which equalled the attack made on the prisoner in Auburn last Sunday.'

The prison authorities issued a denial, but Moulton's story struck a chord with a growing number of New Yorkers who feared that the closed worlds of the prisons concealed terrible abuses. Perry was now an object both of admiration, for his daring, and of pity, for his treatment. A local newspaper editor, defending the prison, feared that Perry would gain new admirers because of the escape and roundly denounced his supporters: 'Is it not about time that Oliver Curtis Perry be treated like the outlaw and desperado he is and not like a hero of the Jesse James stripe of a man?'

Perry was, in fact, doubly punished. As he faced the darkness, silence and starvation of the dungeon for over three weeks, he also knew that his failure had condemned him to serve many more years in prison. For the escape attempt he lost nine years, eleven months and four days of 'good time'. Even if he behaved like a lamb from now on, he would serve at least forty years. A calmer man might have realized that the real battle now was to survive and submit to the regime in the hope of a quieter life, however limited. But Perry was a fighter and was set on a course that would lead to continuous conflict with his keepers.

Over the next few months he was sentenced twice more to spells in the dungeon, for 'insolence and threats to Night Guard', then 'striking keeper, insolence and threats'. Just as he had become increasingly desperate and unruly in Lyons when he realized he could not escape, so now he made life as difficult for his keepers, and for himself, as he could. The perpetual conflict, punctuated by sensory deprivation and near-starvation that weakened his physical condition, took a heavy toll. Perry was not obviously broken, as so many others had been, but the damage had been done. His hostility to authority became ever more extreme and he lost any sense of perspective in his understanding of his own situation. Oliver Perry was under extreme psychological pressure.

There was, briefly, a glimmer of hope by the spring of 1893, when he was sent back to work in the foundry and found what he called 'a little gleam of happiness'. But one violent attack extinguished it. Perry had gradually become convinced that Principal Keeper James Shaw, who had first sent him to the dungeon and ordered most, if not all, of his subsequent punishments, had a serious grudge against him. He believed that Shaw, apart from singling him out for rebuke, was reducing his food rations out of spite. Shaw was a big man with a tough style and, although there is no evidence to suggest he was maliciously inclined towards his prisoner, Perry's fears were not unusual. In the crowded conditions of a prison, fears multiply like germs, and withholding or contaminating food, with saliva or worse, was, and is, an easy way of unofficially punishing a prisoner. A man who, like Perry, had been on starvation rations in the dungeon for long periods might well be particularly anxious about having his fair share of food. But Perry's fear turned to panic.

Isolated from anyone, friends or family, who might help him keep a sense of proportion, he decided that Shaw was out to kill him and resolved to fight back. So he got hold of a file from a workshop and hid it in his uniform until one day he broke ranks and lunged at Shaw. He was immediately overpowered by other keepers and dragged to a dungeon where he was blasted with a high-pressure fire hose until he was subdued. On 11 May 1893, he was judged guilty of 'threats to kill officer and refusal to come out of cell', and was returned to the dungeon. This time he was given a little longer than usual. His sentence was forty-four days, over six weeks.

When he emerged from this terrible punishment it was clear that he had suffered a total breakdown. The anxiety that Shaw was trying to starve him had been magnified into a total paranoia that his keepers had been bribed by a vengeful American Express to starve or poison him. In the isolation of the dungeon, the 'normal' prisoner's obsession with food had been fed by memories of the constant harassing of his family and friends by detectives. The story-teller had spun a new tale that made complete sense to his damaged mind and on his release from the dungeon he was determined to put a stop to the detectives' agents by any means he could.

Eventually, worried about his increasingly violent behaviour, the Warden called for a formal medical examination by Dr Conant Sawyer, the prison physician, and a specialist in 'brain diseases', Dr Frederick Sefton, who confirmed that Perry had 'hallucinations', evidence of an 'unsound mind'. Such was Perry's reputation as a would-be escaper that some observers insisted that he was feigning madness to get a transfer to a less secure institution. The authorities took no notice. On 27 December 1893, after twenty months in Auburn, Perry was officially declared insane and an order was drawn up to transfer him to the Matteawan Asylum for Insane Criminals.

CHAPTER 9

'God forgive us all . . .'

THE PERSONALITY traits and psychological characteristics that contributed to Perry's trauma were quite likely the same ones that had brought him to prison in the first place. In line with the thinking of the day, the doctor who certified him looked for mental illness in his family, citing the fact that his paternal grandmother had been insane. But if his family history had something to reveal, it was a troubled childhood, not a genetic inheritance, which would eventually lead Oliver Perry to the dungeon and despair.

The history has been hard to uncover. The lives of the nineteenth-century rural poor are often elusive. Sometimes names appear in census returns, in church or institutional records, but the lives behind the citations are rarely visible. Perry's boyhood was doubly obscured. When he was a wanted man in the 1890s, detectives had to overcome his family and friends' efforts to cover his traces, but within a matter of decades he was almost entirely expunged from his family's memory. No stories seem to have been told in the Perry family about their black sheep. Even more painfully, while many families have obscured the traces of a bad or mad relative after their deaths, Perry had been repeatedly disowned by his family since birth.

Perry told the same brief story of his early boyhood all his life. His parents, who lived on a farm, separated just a few years after his birth, when his mother left. He said he was born on 17 September, but gave the year as 1865 and 1866 in different accounts. His father, the outwardly respectable but slippery Oliver H. Perry, was a native New Yorker, one of thirteen children born to a farmer. In January 1865, at the age of nineteen, he married a fifteen-year-old called Mary Allen. She was the daughter of a widowed farmer who had married Oliver's own, equally young sister, Sarah Emily. They lived in what was known as the 'Irish Settlement', near a Mohawk Valley township named Ephratah after the biblical land of plenty. There, just over eight months later, Oliver Curtis Perry was born.

The only fact about his mother that Oliver Perry ever recalled was that when he was a very small boy she left him and his father and never came back. No one knows why she left or where she went. She simply disappeared from public, and private, records; she may have married again or, as some reports hinted, died soon afterwards, but she left no traces. Oliver H. Perry soon married again. His new wife, Sarah, was, like Mary and his sister, fifteen years old at the time of her marriage and first pregnancy. Blanche, Oliver's half-sister, was born in 1872.

When her own child was born, Sarah wanted a home of her own and insisted that there would be no place in it for her stepson. No reason was ever given. Perhaps she was insecure about her husband's feelings for his first wife and took it out on their son. In adulthood Perry would poignantly stress that his father had 'insisted' on keeping him, but in fact he offered little resistance to his wife's plan. Perry's grandmother looked after him for a while but when she died he had nobody to turn to. The little boy was effectively alone in the world.

A signpost still points the way to the Irish Settlement. When Perry was born it was a community of small farms worked mainly, as the name suggests, by those of Irish descent. The poor soil offered only a basic living, and when competition came from the opening up of western farmlands, many were forced to seek a second income at the nearby timber mills. Today the tarmac road soon dwindles to a dirt track, with woods thickening and closing in on either side. But there is no sign of farms or houses. All that remains of the settlement where dozens of families worked the land, and where Perry spent the first years of his life, is a few barely visible walls, none more than a few stones high, overgrown with ivy and brambles. Looking closer, it is possible to see the broken outlines of houses spaced alongside the road. Within a few decades, the Irish Settlement, a living community, had been reclaimed by the woods that once provided its timber. The speed with which human attempts to make a home can be undone, not by war or demolition but by the gradual, relentless reclamation of nature, is both surprising and moving.

The Irish Settlement today.

The wild wood, one of the most abiding and unsettling locations of childhood fantasies and terrors, is a fitting symbol of Perry's earliest years. In fairytales it is the testing ground for children who roam too far and find themselves alone and frightened by the unknown. Traditionally, in the end, lost children learn their lessons and return safely home to their family. In Perry's case, the wood has overwhelmed the home, as once the tangled relationships of his family left him lost and rejected. Unable to find a place where he felt at home, he would spend the rest of his childhood wandering.

His aunt Mary wrote about her family's guilt in a letter to a newspaper when Perry was awaiting trial: 'God forgive us all for our negligence in not taking care of him in his helplessness. . . . He was turned out on the charity of the world, when, if we had taken him in, all would have been well with him.' But none of his family would take him in, so before he was ten years old, he was almost certainly left in what was known as an 'orphan asylum', although he had both a father and a stepmother living. The impact on a little boy is hard to measure. Intriguingly, in the Depression years Louis Berg, whose *Confessions of a Prison Doctor* argued passionately for reform in the treatment of offenders and for an understanding of the impact of broken homes on young children, would call those who turned to crime because of being unwanted, 'stepchildren of society'.

Perry later referred to working on a farm from the age of eleven. He was probably left in an orphanage or refuge and 'adopted', as so many children were, to provide slave labour. Nobody is sure where Perry was left, although a newspaper report in 1892 identified a likely place in upstate New York where names he later supposedly used as aliases were popular. He soon ran away from his adopted home, as resentful of working for nothing as he would later be in prison.

By the summer of 1880 he had travelled to Minnesota and was staying with his aunt Mary. She and her husband Edward had moved from New York to the sparsely populated Otter Tail County where they farmed and ran a small general store in a village called Luce. His aunt described a sensitive, kind boy: 'He was naturally kind and tender-hearted, but, as I said before, circumstances made him what he is. He has been known to give his last ten cents to a little beggar girl . . . who was (as he thought) in more need than he was, although he had no place to lay his head.'

But by the age of fourteen he had left Minnesota. It is not clear whether he was sent away or left of his own accord. His aunt's sense of guilt may suggest that he was sent away, but he may have been simply restless and homesick. As he later commented, 'I was a headstrong boy, and have had a blot on my whole life.'

By the winter of 1881 he was back in upstate New York, sleeping rough. His father lived in a village called Amboy in Oswego County with his second family, including eight-year-old Blanche and a six-year-old son, Claude. Neighbours remembered his elder son visiting occasionally, but never staying long. Perry clearly wanted to belong, but his family's relative indifference and his own restlessness left him perpetually unsettled. His step-mother had made it clear he was not part of her family, and his father, with the responsibility of his new family, had little time for his first-born son.

Oliver Perry was forced to be a man when he was still a little boy and he had no reason to trust anyone. His mother had abandoned him, his grandmother had died, and what could he expect from a father whose love and protection were so unreliable? Little wonder that as a grown man he would have such troubled relationships and see betrayal even before it happened. Or that he would grow up determined to prove himself, to win the acceptance and admiration, if not affection, that he had been denied. Underneath the clever robber and slick self-inventor who charmed the press and public was a deeply insecure little boy.

Unwanted, he took to a life of what he later called 'roving'. He learned early how to handle a gun, as many country boys did. He travelled alone, around the Mohawk valley where he would one day hide from his pursuers, and further afield. To survive, he learned how to live by his wits, if not always within the law.

CHAPTER 10

A Bad Boy's Career

O NE C O L D November day in 1881 Oliver Perry was arrested in the city of Amsterdam in the eastern Mohawk valley. Two boys had reported him to the police for stealing a new suit of clothes from a man at the railroad depot. He was alone, homeless and had to pay for shelter. He was held in the lock-up over the weekend, tried, found guilty, and sentenced to an institution that was called, with bitter irony, the Western House of Refuge.

It was located in Rochester, the city just south of Lake Ontario where the adult Perry would one day appear in wax. Today the gleaming new towers of Rochester's optical and photographic industries dwarf its older buildings, creating an impression of bland modernity and affluence. But right through its heart runs the deep gorge of the Genessee River, a reminder of a rugged, ancient landscape.

The House of Refuge was itself originally established as a progressive institution, but by 1881 it was at best an over-crowded, ill-disciplined prison, at worst a hellish place where young children were subjected to physical, psychological and sexual abuse by their fellow inmates and, all too frequently, by their keepers.

Newspaper reports from the years when Perry was an inmate make shocking reading. Time and again the Board of Managers, comprising eminent local citizens, condemned the institution. In 1883 it was denounced as 'brutal in the extreme', and a year later the *New York Times* noted that 'the most cruel and inhuman treatment has been inflicted upon the boys'. An official investigation found that brutality was widespread and possibly systematic. Witnesses reported beatings with rulers, paddles, strops and sticks, as well as a key used to twist children's noses and ears. Even when 'properly' administered, punishment was harsh. Children found guilty of rule-breaking, including whispering or failing to meet work targets, were punished by beating or starvation rations of bread and water. If Perry had experienced hardship as a roving boy, the privations in the Refuge were worse. One eleven-year-old boy was put on a bread-and-water diet for four weeks.

Boys who tried to escape or were insubordinate would be stripped and locked up in dark cells, not unlike the dungeons in Auburn, with boarded-up windows and a heavy door with a few ventilation holes. The existence of the rat-infested cells was initially concealed from the Board of Managers, but was eventually revealed by witnesses, including a boy who had been held in one for six months. An investigator who entered a dark cell had to leave immediately, driven out by the stench from the waste bucket that served as the boy's lavatory and would be emptied only once a day, if the keeper was diligent. In these dreadful cells boys slept naked, except for a blanket, on the floor. Conditions were little better in the regular dormitories, with open waste buckets and no lavatory paper. Unsurprisingly, the Board worried that boys were 'acquiring the most filthy personal habits without fault on their part'. Could this be why Perry was so fastidious in later life, when many reporters commented on his almost obsessive need to keep his hands clean?

There may have been another, more disturbing, trigger for his need to cleanse himself. Apart from the hard labour, locked fire-escapes, poor food, filth and summary punishments, the boys faced another threat: sexual abuse. One employee made extensive, albeit coyly worded, accusations of 'immoral practices' on the part not only of boys but also of their keepers. Perry, even as a grown man, was delicate in stature and looks, described by the Pinkertons as 'effeminate'. When he was admitted to the refuge he was small for his age. He was fifteen or even sixteen, depending on his real birth year, but as records show, he was only 4 feet $11\frac{3}{4}$ inches tall and weighed $91\frac{3}{4}$ pounds, and so a likely target for sexual predators. Years later, he would complain bitterly of how young men were systematically sexually abused by older convicts, but in his youth there was nobody to turn to. So he concentrated on gaining some weight and building up his strength. This was clearly designed to help him defend himself, to turn a slight boy who might be treated as a girl into a man. He certainly learned a style of fighting – scratching and biting – that would stay with him all his life. Whenever he felt overpowered, particularly by a bigger man, Oliver Perry would fight frantically, almost hysterically, like a little boy.

The exact nature of Perry's experiences in the House of Refuge will never be known but they certainly shaped his character and established a pattern of response to prison that would last a lifetime. He must have found the institution almost unendurable, even without the additional torments of punishment and abuse. Used to a life on the road that, despite its hardships, was free, the confinement alone would have been wretched. Living rough as a boy-man he had learned to conceal his vulnerability beneath a tough, clever manner that seemed like impudence and brought out the worst in his keepers. When chastised he resorted to running away, as he had done as a child. Escape was almost a compulsion for a boy who had no reason to believe that there was any other way of learning to live within the rules in an unfair system. In his desperate plotting to escape he demonstrated, even at this early stage, two defining characteristics that would be seen again and again in his adult life: the extraordinary intelligence and ingenuity that would make his crimes and escapes so remarkable, and the charismatic charm that would allow him to exert an almost mesmerizing influence over fellow prisoners, hardened reporters and ordinary Americans.

His keepers, infuriated by his conduct, wanted him moved to an adult prison. In 1883 one wrote to the Superintendent:

The boy has always been a vulgar and low dispositioned boy, and of late his disregard of all advice makes me call your especial attention to his case. He has never cared for his studies and his whole general deportment has been low and vulgar. He is constantly reported for disorder, quarrelling, impudence and vulgar actions and language. . . . Lately he has been engaged in altering and picking locks and in attempting to escape till his example and acts are so bold and defiant that his removal from this institution is quite a necessity. Quite recently he secured false keys with which he let himself out of his dormitory in the night time and broke his way through the shop, stealing therefrom knives and weapons of defence but was unable to scale the walls. Certainly his low and vile disposition with no intention to reform exerts a very dangerous and pernicious influence over the other inmates.

Intriguingly, the expertise with making false keys that would emerge in Lyons seems to have been evident while he was still a boy.

To his keepers Perry was simply a bad lot, but an investigation into the institution revealed that some of his accusers were guilty of worse. One was dismissed for cruelty and incompetence, and another was reported by a witness to have given a newly admitted boy fifty strokes with a rattan cane. Yet another later became an officer in the police force and joined in the hunt for Perry after his second train robbery. After his capture Perry was anxious to show he had not intended to hurt anyone, but he made one exception. He swore publicly that if he had been able to get a clear shot at the ex-keeper he would have killed him.

The keepers' request to have Perry transferred was granted. On 7 March 1883 he was sent to the Monroe County penitentiary 'for correction during the pleasure of the Board of Managers for a period not exceeding two years'. There his behaviour followed the same pattern as in the Refuge, but one dramatic incident revealed a particular facet of his personality that would later become almost as defining as his need to escape.

When he arrived he was put to work as a heel trimmer in a workshop where convicts laboured for a shoe-making company. He struck up a relationship with the keeper in charge of the workshop, a man called Kelly, who felt sorry for a boy stuck in a men's prison and sometimes shared his lunch with Perry. But when Perry was transferred to work on a machine rather than with the trimming knife, he was discovered sabotaging it, presumably because he had hoped to use the knife in an escape attempt. Publicly reprimanded by Kelly, he grabbed up a skiving knife, used for trimming leather, and lunged at the keeper as he would later lunge at Shaw in Auburn.

When his punishment was complete, he was transferred to another workshop but took the chance, when sent to Kelly on an errand, to attack the man who had frustrated his plans. This time he created a diversion by shouting to the other prisoners to get out and creating a stampede. In the chaos he seemed torn between trying to escape and getting his own back on Kelly. When the panic subsided Kelly had a cut on his arm and Perry a stab wound in the stomach, described in official reports as accidentally self-inflicted. He was taken to the prison infirmary and then into solitary confinement for the remainder of his sentence.

When he left the penitentiary on 15 March 1885, at the age of nineteen, Perry had acquired a range of skills, in shoe-making, lock-picking, improvising weapons and fighting. He had learned that he could influence and manipulate others, but could also find himself at their mercy. An intelligent but volatile young man, he could be charming and aggressive by turns. He had entered the House of Refuge as an unruly boy who longed for affection and belonging but chafed against restrictions; three-and-a-half years later he left the penitentiary as a young man with a deep hatred of authority and confinement. And he had clearly decided that the best response to both was to fight, with whatever resources he had. He had also developed a pattern of behaviour that would mark the rest of his life and involved a series of men who might be seen as father figures.

The testimony of the Monroe keepers suggests that he forged a number of close relationships with keepers. These were men in authority whose approval and affection he craved but whom, ultimately, he could not trust and whose attempts to discipline him provoked his most extreme reactions. Another workshop overseer claimed, like Kelly, to have liked the difficult prisoner.

He told reporters that 'young Perry had a particular liking for me and would do almost anything to please me', and that the young man had come to his house for dinner after his release. It is quite possible that there was a sexual dimension to the relationships, and the men's descriptions of their relations with the young boy sound very like those given by men who 'groom' children as potential sexual partners. They may have been genuinely sympathetic, but, whatever their motives, Perry was almost certainly unconsciously trying to re-create his relationship with his own father. Later, in Lyons, the gentle Sheriff Thornton and tougher Deputy Collins embodied different aspects of the father, one offering support, the other punishment. His own father had alternately owned and disowned him, leaving his son locked in a perpetual battle with authority. Again and again, he would turn to a keeper, a lawman or a doctor for support and understanding, only to feel betrayed and abandoned. This would lead, in turn, to intolerably disruptive behaviour that ultimately would become self-destructive.

Oliver H. Perry was still ambivalent about his son. He claimed later that he tried to secure Perry's release from Monroe and although he had not fought for him in childhood, it seems he sometimes intervened in emergencies, as he would again in 1892, when he concealed his fugitive son and later tried to help him escape from jail. Like many badly behaved children, Perry must have unconsciously known that breaking the rules brought him the rewards of parental attention. As he grew up, did the same impulse lie behind the ever greater risks he took and the ever more daring crimes he committed?

Initially Perry tried to settle down to an honest life, getting a job as a clerk in a Rochester shoe store. The storekeeper remembered him as a pleasant-looking young man, a 'great talker' and a bit 'fly', although generally reliable. But he soon found the settled life difficult and after three or four months gave in his notice.

In the following spring he was in trouble again, this time for stealing from his own family. Together with some other men, he broke into his uncle's store in Minnesota and stole money from the till, some revolvers and clothes. The other men, who he said were army deserters, escaped but Perry, who stayed around assuming he would not be suspected, was followed, searched and arrested. He was sentenced to two years' hard labour in Stillwater prison. His sympathetic aunt believed that he had been harshly punished because he would not betray his 'pards', but he seemed unconcerned about betraying his own family's trust. Perhaps this was understandable, given his history. Anticipating the justification of his later robbery by condemning an exploitative system, he claimed he was just taking what was owed him for working for his uncle as a boy.

Stillwater was one of the mid-west's best-known prisons, but less for its tough regime than for its famous inmates. Here, the young man who would become the most famous train robber in the east encountered the west's most notorious living outlaws: Cole, Jim and Bob Younger who, with Frank and Jesse James, had terrorized the west in the aftermath of the Civil War, robbing trains and banks. Although Perry later remembered them, they do not seem to have impressed him much. All three were model prisoners, while Perry was as rebellious in Stillwater as he had been in Monroe.

He was released in the summer of 1888 when he was twenty-two. Then, probably fuelled by tales told by Stillwater inmates, he headed further west. The west may have been tamer in the late

1880s, but it was still a wild place where the rules of eastern society rarely applied. Here a man could move more freely, on cattle trails and railroads, and pick up casual jobs where few questions were asked, a definite help to an ex-prisoner and especially appealing to a young man who hated regulation. But the boundaries between legality and criminality, even between lawman and outlaw, were also less secure, and Perry almost certainly crossed the line.

He gave varying but always vague accounts of this period of his life, when he would have met his doomed sweetheart on a ranch in New Mexico. He certainly worked in the west, as a cowboy and ranch hand, and got into bad company. The Pinkertons believed that he learned the basics of train robbery at this time, and he later claimed to have been in a gang who operated in Texas, Nebraska and the Chicago area. He never gave any details, nor did the Pinkertons, and when he robbed the American Express Special he worked alone, using methods unlike those of any gang. It is possible that he was embellishing, just as others tried to pin unsolved crimes on him, but there may have been a gang whose story has been lost for ever. One thing is certain: in the precious months he spent in the west, Perry was a free man.

But sometime in 1888 or 1889 he decided to move back to New York. He later claimed, and Amelia Haswell believed, that this was because he had fallen in love and hoped to earn money to buy a home for his forbidden sweetheart. But there may have been another catalyst for his decision to end his roving life and settle down.

The Perry family clearly had a strained relationship with their wayward elder son. But as 1888 drew to a close, it was his half-sister Blanche who was in the news. Just before Christmas the fifteen-year-old girl was shot dead on the snowy sidewalk outside her father's house by her estranged husband, William Crossley, who then turned the gun on himself. The couple had been childhood sweethearts, then fallen out when Crossley headed west to make a fortune but returned, broke, bitter and sure that his beautiful young wife had been unfaithful.

The murder and suicide made sensational news, especially as the funerals of husband and wife both took place on Boxing Day, with Blanche buried in the Perry family plot and William in the Crossley grave, facing each other in perpetual accusation across a narrow path in the same cemetery.

Perry was not listed as being present at his half-sister's funeral but he may well have been incognito, if he was still in trouble with the law. He may not have been in New York at the time, of course, but the date of Blanche's murder coincides intriguingly with the timing of his apparent decision to start life again in Troy after his western wildness. The coincidence certainly offers an alternative to the story of Perry's doomed New Mexican romance as the reason for his decision to return to New York. His choice of alias when arrested – William Cross, so near to William Crossley – was surely not a coincidence. Why would a young man adopt a version of the name of the killer of his own sister? Was it an act of revenge, or a sign of his guilt about his own strained relationship with his family? While he was waiting for his trial he wrote to his father: 'If anything should happen to me I want to be buried alongside of dear Blanchy.' It is hard at a distance to know if this and his other affectionate references to his little brother 'Claudy' were genuine signs of strong family feeling or displays of expected sentiment.

Intriguingly, if less attractively, Blanche may also have played another part in her stepbrother's life after her death. Descriptions of her striking dark looks resemble uncannily those of the girl in the photograph he carried and whom Amelia Haswell believed to be his dead sweetheart. Photographs and jewellery with locks of hair were popular mementos of dead relatives. It may have been a coincidence and Perry's sweetheart may have been real. But the similarity begs a probably unanswerable question. Faced with a struggle to win sympathy after his crimes had been discovered, and needing the support of his devout but romantic 'Mother', had the ever-resourceful Perry used his sister's image to spin a tale?

As ever, Perry is infuriatingly difficult to pin down, alternately crying out to be read, as he was by the Pinkertons, as a cynical manipulator of other people's naïve or idealistic beliefs, or, as he was by his Christian and liberal supporters, as a damaged boy whose kinder, more thoughtful nature was crushed by his inability to cope with a brutal system. In truth, he was probably both, the product of a troubled childhood and a brutal adolescence that would turn him into a daring but volatile rebel, capable of sensitivity but also of ruthlessness. His was a personality that would both lead him to prison and make him particularly vulnerable to its impact.

Whether affected by a forbidden romance or a family tragedy, by 1890 he had decided to try conformity, working on the railroad, becoming part of a community. But disillusionment with the poor rewards and petty restrictions of his new life had swiftly driven him to prove his ability and his worth as an outlaw. For a few months he had experienced the intoxicating excitement, unprecedented luxury and strange, hunted freedom of his life as a wanted man. Finally, in Auburn, confined and isolated, his highly strung nature had been stretched to breaking-point.

CHAPTER II

'Came to Hell'

THE MATTEAWAN Asylum for Insane Criminals, daunting as it sounds, offered Perry a glimmer of hope. Staying in Auburn would undoubtedly have doomed him to decline or possible suicide. In the asylum, much nearer Troy, it would be easier for Amelia Haswell and Perry's other old friends to visit him and offer some emotional support. Although breakdowns induced by the stress of isolation are traumatic, they are rarely permanent. In more stable and secure conditions, given a chance to build reliable relationships with other people, even those with extreme psychotic symptoms can recover and may never experience another episode.

On 28 December 1893, one day after he was declared insane, Perry, looking pale and thin, was escorted by three armed guards on the long train journey from Auburn to Matteawan. Word spread quickly among the passengers and soon the car he was in was crowded. But anyone expecting to see the famous showman put on an act, or to hear the ravings of a madman, was disappointed. Perry was unusually quiet as the journey took him back along the tracks of his robberies, through the landscape of his childhood, hugging the course of the Hudson River until, the following morning, the guards escorted him through the crowds and into a carriage and headed for the asylum.

An imposing building on a hill just outside the small community of Beacon, Matteawan was New York State's institution for prisoners who had been certified insane after sentencing. It had been open for just over a year. On 25 April 1892 crowds of villagers had watched the first sixty prisoners arrive in chains. Newspapers of the time noted that while some were in straitjackets, others carried personal possessions including birdcages. They had all been held in the previous State Asylum for Insane Criminals, near Auburn prison, whose location was far from ideal, with incessant noise from nearby factories. The State Commissioner in Lunacy, Dr Carlos F. MacDonald, argued that the insane should be put to farm work in the open air, and campaigned for the foundation of a more suitable asylum. Eventually, the state legislature voted to pay for a new institution at Matteawan, whose rural location offered peace and fresh air. To many people, the insane were still objects of fear and scorn, the criminal insane even worse, so at its inception Matteawan must have seemed liberal indeed.

Local feelings were mixed. The asylum offered much-needed employment, but the idea of insane criminals breaking loose filled many with dread. Despite reassurances about security, within three months of the opening several 'patients' had escaped and there were persistent rumours about would-be escapees feigning insanity in order to get into, then out of, the hospital. Now a man who had publicly declared his intention not to serve his sentence, who had repeatedly shown he had the initiative and nerve to break out, and who had nearly escaped from Auburn, was arriving. Even in the Certificate of Lunacy the physician Conant

Sawyer had warned, 'he is a bad desperate man and you cannot be too careful, or he may well escape from your place'. The man in charge, Medical Superintendent Dr Henry Allison, knew he had something to prove.

Dr Henry Allison.

Allison was an urbane New Englander, born in Concord, New Hampshire in 1851, who trained in medicine after reading classics at Dartmouth College. He started his medical career at the Willard State Hospital in Seneca County, New York before taking up a position at Auburn and then at Matteawan. He had been warned by Auburn officials that Perry would be troublesome, but laughed, 'I guess he'll get on all right here.' Perry also seemed initially optimistic about the hospital and its Superintendent. On arrival, he held out his hand to Allison, saying, 'You are a man and a gentleman. I can tell it by looking at you. I am glad to come here if you are in charge, for I know you will treat me well. You have a kindly face; you have no idea how different it is from those I have left. My God, I hope I never have to go back there again, to be beaten and starved and poisoned.'

He repeated his hopes to a reporter who was allowed to interview him soon after his arrival. The newsman was shocked at the change in Perry's looks since his trial, describing him as pale and thin, with sunken cheeks and the hair at the back of his head worn thin. But he thought that apart from insisting on his persecution by Auburn officers, Perry seemed fairly rational as he spoke of how friends would see his situation: 'Yes, I have a great many friends outside, and I want them to hear that I'm all right.

Tell them I'm glad to be just where I am, too. They'll wonder at that, won't they? Don't think for a moment that I don't know where I am, young man. I'm in a lunatic asylum, but better far to be in an asylum, than in that cursed prison. . . . Perry in a madhouse. It makes me laugh to think of it. And my laugh is a treat to me. I thought I should never laugh again after I had been at Auburn for a time.'

Once more Perry hoped to make a good impression on a figure of authority and a fresh start in a new place, but while it was a relief from Auburn, the regime in Matteawan would not be to his liking. After an interview with Dr Allison, he was immediately sent to a cell on an isolation ward. The ward was in a separate building, connected to the main block by a long corridor. There the most unruly and dangerous inmates were held in separate cells where a system of sliding doors allowed guards to watch them, unseen, at any time of day or night. This enabled them not only to check for signs of normality in prisoners faking insanity but also to guard those prisoners who, like Perry, were most likely to attempt to escape. It is not difficult to imagine his reaction.

If this disheartened Perry, the Superintendent's views on insanity would have plunged him into total despair. Although the men and women in Matteawan were still convicts, they were called 'patients' in recognition of their illness. But these patients had little hope of being cured, even if their current condition was one that would today be judged temporary. Edward Meredith, committed two years earlier because of a 'delusion', like Perry's of being poisoned, had, exceptionally, been able to prove his sanity and won his freedom, but only after a lengthy court battle with the prison and hospital authorities. In practice few patients ever returned to complete their sentences in prison. As an alienist, a specialist in mental disorders, Henry Allison took his role in caring for individual patients seriously, but he recognized that his role was also to contain those who threatened the social order.

The closing decades of the nineteenth century may have seen great changes in the treatment of the insane generally, with increasingly professional psychiatric approaches adopted in purpose-built institutions, but insane criminals were, above all, a threat to be contained. Shortly after Perry arrived in Matteawan, Dr Allison addressed the American Medico-Psychological Association at its annual conference and his paper, 'Insanity among Criminals', was published in the Association's influential *Journal of Insanity*. In the article he described men with mental disturbance very much like Perry's and argued that even when they are 'no longer insane, in the strict meaning of the term', they are 'in a condition which is recognized as unsoundness of mind', 'not amenable to prison discipline and are incorrigible'. Such prisoners should, he argued, be kept in hospital for an 'indeterminate sentence'. He concluded that by committing the insane 'for life', the judiciary and medical professions would succeed in 'permanently ridding society of many dangerous and undesirable elements'.

So while a public still in love with his romantic past wondered if Perry was shamming, he and his friends must have feared that he was now condemned to perpetual imprisonment. His escape attempts had lost him his remission, but while his sentence had a time limit, he had hope. If he recovered psychologically, he could, one day, be free. But would the Superintendent ever judge him eligible? There are no available records to reveal Henry Allison's original assessment of Perry. But the patient made his feelings plain on his cell wall. Below his name and the date, he wrote, 'CAME TO HELL'.

CHAPTER 12

Lunatics on a Rampage

IN APRIL 1895 Perry took everyone by surprise once more. In the eighteen months since his transfer from Auburn he had been regularly treated for unruly behaviour but his overall condition seemed to improve. Amelia Haswell had welcomed the chance to visit him in the more conveniently located institution but was often told he was too ill to see her. When she did get to see him, he complained about his cell in the isolation ward, the behaviour of the keepers and doctors, and of being prevented from taking any exercise in the fresh air. Amelia complained to Dr Allison, but Perry decided to take more direct action.

Just after 11 o'clock on the night of 10 April a watchman on his usual round walked towards the isolation ward. Checking here was really a formality. The isolation ward was a prison within a prison, designed to prevent escapes. So its outer walls had a lining of sheet-iron between two layers of brick, its windows were secured by iron bars and galvanized wire shutters, and the ceilings had even been secured with stone flagging. The cells had been constructed just as carefully. The doors were made of two-inch-thick oak and each had two locks, specially designed so that they could only be turned from the outside. As a final security measure, the keepers who held the keys were bound by the strictest orders never to take them outside the prison. Any man who did so was risking instant dismissal.

The watchman walked briskly along the corridor to the only door into the isolation ward. On either side, just before the door, were rooms used by the ward attendants. As he passed by, both were quiet, as he expected. At this time of night most of the prison attendants were asleep. He unlocked the door, entered the ward and was about to start checking the cell doors when he heard someone calling him from a cell at the far end. It was Perry. The train robber, who was housed in one of six cells that stood at a right angle to those along the length of the ward, was a demanding patient. Only the day before he had complained about being disturbed by noise from workmen in the nearby chapel and had asked when he could expect some peace. He was told the work would finish in a couple of days.

'What's the matter in there?' called the watchman. Perry asked for water. As the watchman started to turn away, three men pounced. One grabbed his keys while the others held him down. Before he could cry out, someone placed a hand over his mouth. He was bundled into Perry's cell, then tied to the bed-frame with strips of torn sheet. One of the men stuffed his mouth with rags and his attackers rushed out of the cell.

While he struggled in Perry's cell, its former occupant, together with the watchman's other assailants, Patrick Maguire and John Quigley, and two other men, Frank Davis and Michael O'Donnell, whom they released en route, unlocked the ward door, then locked it again behind them. They crept past the attendants' rooms and down the corridor. At the far end were stairs to the prison chapel, one of a very few parts of the prison, outside the ward, with which these 'isolation' prisoners were familiar. They unlocked the doors at the foot and top of the stairs with the watchman's keys. In the darkness

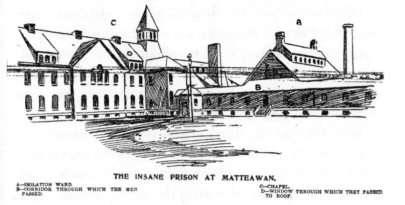

THE INSANE PRISON AT MATTEAWAN.

A—ISOLATION WARD.
B—CORRIDOR THROUGH WHICH THE MEN PASSED.
C—CHAPEL.
D—WINDOW THROUGH WHICH THEY PASSED TO ROOF.

Matteawan State Hospital.

they could just discern what they were looking for. At one end of the room was a step-ladder, left by workmen repairing the ceiling. Maguire had seen it at a service he attended – to his keepers' amazement – in preparation for some patients' confirmation by the Bishop of Albany. He had told Perry, who complained about the noise, to discover how long the ladder would be in place. Now Perry and his companions climbed twenty-five feet to the top of the ladder, pulled themselves up through a small hatch in the ceiling, and disappeared.

They crawled on hands and knees along the dusty attic floor until they reached a dormer window. No one had thought it necessary to secure an attic window above a double-locked chapel. The glass was easily broken and the men slipped through the window and out on to guttering along the eaves, forty feet above the ground. They edged along the guttering to the front of the building, then shinned down a pair of iron drainpipes. Someone shouted 'Halt!' and a shot rang out. A watchman stationed outside had spotted them and fired in their direction. The men kept on running and the watchman rushed inside to raise the alarm.

127

Dr Allison ordered men to surround the building to prevent any further escapes. Inside, the whole asylum was in uproar, as keepers and prisoners woke to cries of 'Escape!' Keepers still half-asleep emerged from their rooms and ran along the corridors, but nobody knew who had escaped. Eventually, men ran to the isolation ward and discovered the truth.

Soon police officers, detectives and local inhabitants were on the lookout for the fugitive lunatics. The moon, appropriately enough, was full, and the bright light made the searchers optimistic. The men were all wearing the asylum uniform of grey pants and vests, grey coats and blue and white striped hickory shirts. While their uniform would be an obvious give-away, they had another, more immediate problem. The men held in the isolation ward of the asylum were judged too dangerous to be allowed to wear shoes. They were on the run in felt slippers or barefoot. Surely they could not get far? But despite an all-night search, no trace was found of the five men.

The following morning Allison took stock of the situation and prepared a statement for the press. Any escape was embarrassing, but this was particularly humiliating. Most of what had happened was pieced together easily enough. The men had obviously planned the escape after seeing the workmen's ladder in the chapel when attending Sunday service, and had used the watchman's keys to free their companions and then unlock the ward door. But one question remained unanswered. How had Perry and the others got out of their cells in the first place? Their fellow inmates were being interrogated, but if any were sane enough to give answers that made sense, they were not doing so.

The Superintendent candidly announced that the only explanation was that an asylum employee must have colluded in the escape.

Although he refused to speculate, the newspapers all reported that the watchman had been suspended from duty and was being questioned. To help in the hunt, Allison's Deputy, Dr Robert Lamb, supplied the police with recent photographs of the escapees. Lamb was a keen amateur photographer and had jumped at the chance of testing his skills by developing pictures from negatives in his own darkroom. The pictures were sent to the police in all major cities and to American Express, whose representative rushed to Matteawan. Perry may have been paranoid about the company persecuting him but he was not wrong about their continued interest. They still wanted their missing money and they were still determined he should suffer the full penalty for his crimes.

Little is known about Perry's fellow fugitives. Three were burglars whose 'insanity' had evidently not prevented them from joining Perry in planning and executing a very complicated escape: Davis, the oldest at forty-two, was serving twenty-five years for burglary; Maguire, known as 'Ugly Mac', was a forty-year-old housebreaker who had made several escape attempts in the past; O'Donnell was the youngest at twenty-five and had eleven years of a sentence for burglary left to serve. John Quigley was a rather different case. He had been in trouble since childhood and seems to have had a life of extraordinary misfortune that left him seriously disturbed. After a series of petty crimes, he shot and killed his mother in what the Coroner's jury decided was an accident. Soon afterwards, he was shot through the ear while being arrested for breaking into a woman's house and criminally assaulting her and was sentenced to fifteen years in Sing-Sing. There his behaviour resulted in a move to Matteawan where, like the others, he met the persuasive Perry and became involved in the escape.

While the hunt spread out across the surrounding countryside,

John Quigley.

everyone tried to work out where Perry would head. Most agreed he would make his way to a city and possibly seek out one of the wealthy and influential friends of whom he sometimes boasted.

Two days after the escape, on Good Friday, the first fugitive was caught: the pathetic and confused John Quigley who had been utterly unable to cope with life on the run. He was found by local men near an empty freight car, still in uniform, begging for food, and returned to Matteawan without a struggle.

His account of the escape, when interrogated, answered some questions. It also had many echoes of Perry's past escape plans, in Lyons and even Rochester. The keys the convicts used to open the cell doors had, he said, been made from prison spoons. In the isolation ward men judged too dangerous to go to the dining room ate with an iron spoon, as knives or forks could be used as weapons. Patrick Maguire, one of these men, had not only managed to hide two spoons but also, Quigley claimed, used his past experience as a jeweller to turn a thin strip of tempered steel inside the sole of his prison slipper into a saw. Then he transformed the malleable spoons into keys to fit the cell doors; although each cell had two locks, top and bottom, the same two keys would unlock any of the cells on the corridor. Quigley could not explain how Maguire had got the impressions of the locks but it was assumed that a prisoner allowed in the corridor had helped.

Maguire had then apparently slipped the key to the bottom lock through the small aperture in the cell door to one of these milder prisoners, Frank Davis, as he walked along the corridor. On the day of the escape, Davis unlocked the bottom lock of Maguire's cell on his way to supper. When the watchman came to inspect the ward soon afterwards everything seemed quiet. Although he was officially supposed to check every single lock, he rarely did so. After he had gone, Maguire used his improvised saw to cut through two strands of the heavy wire mesh that covered the peephole in his cell door. This allowed him to bend down the mesh, stick his arm through and turn his key in the upper lock. He swung the door open quietly and crept to Davis's cell. Davis passed the other key through to Maguire who released him. Next they released

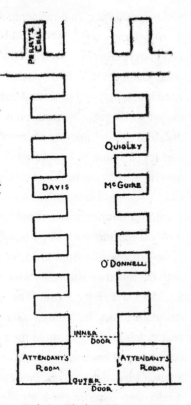

Isolation Block in Matteawan State Hospital.

Perry. Then all three returned to their own cells, pulled the doors to and waited for the watchman's next round.

While Quigley settled back into the relative security of confinement, it seemed that Perry had also returned to familiar territory. A number of storekeepers reported seeing him in Troy, a not unlikely place for him to seek sanctuary. The city's press was, on the whole, still sympathetic to Perry, one reporter summing up the general feeling that his recent escape proved that his 'courage, persistence and ingenuity are qualities which would have made him successful in an honest career'. Sympathetic as Troy might be, sightings of Perry were also reported across the state in any place where a connection with his past could be made. A mysterious man in a sombrero appeared in several villages, leading to rumours that the expert in disguise had adopted a new image. A woman asking questions about him was assumed to be a past lover and a confused man even confessed to being Perry. Perry was everywhere and nowhere to be seen. As one editor succinctly explained, 'Oliver Curtis Perry is a criminal who in two senses is literally out of sight.'

In an attempt to hasten his capture Governor Levi P. Morton took the unusual and dramatic step of proclaiming that the State of New York would offer a $1,000 reward for his arrest. Together with the rewards offered by American Express, this put a bounty of $2,250 on Perry's head. The sum was quite astonishing. Dr Allison's generous annual salary was $3,000, and the reward was much more than most men could hope to earn in a year. In contrast, the reward for each of the other men was $250. Once again, railroad detectives, Pinkerton agents and the press rushed to outdo each other in the hunt for this most wanted man.

Patrick Maguire and Michael O'Donnell were captured soon after Quigley, about forty miles from the asylum. Like Quigley they were weakened by hunger and exposure in the cold spring nights. Now only Perry and Davis, who was regarded as the most dangerous of the other fugitives, were at large. A rumour spread that they might be travelling together, disguised as tramps. This made life even harder than usual for innocent men who were living on the road, some of whom were harassed and even arrested. But Frank Davis was caught alone, after five days on the run. He put up more of a fight than the others, running until shots were fired. Perhaps out of some sort of respect, or pity, his captors plied him with whisky and took him back to Matteawan roaring drunk.

Now only Perry was free. Dr Allison announced that he was confident he would be back in custody within twenty-four hours. Sure enough, on 16 April a newspaper headline declared 'Perry Caught'. But the item continued 'Buying velvet capes at $6.50 and $7 at the New York Cloak and Fur Coats Store, No. 49 east Main Street, on easy payments of $1 or 50c weekly. No collectors.' As the initial fears about escaped lunatics subsided, and recollections of the earlier, charming Perry filled the papers, his capture had become a joke.

Perry's escape was remarkable, not just in his ingenuity in getting out of a specially designed double prison, but also because he was still officially considered a 'madman'. It was clear that Perry had planned the escape with as much intelligence and care as his earlier attempts and executed it with more success. And he had obviously built up strong enough relationships with the other men to earn, and return, their trust. Oliver Perry might be certified insane, but what was his real condition?

Patrick Maguire.

Michael O'Donnell.

Frank Davis.

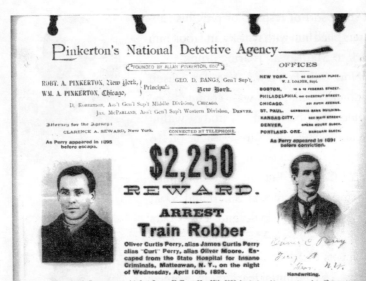

1895 Reward poster (Reproduced from the collection of the Library of Congress).

CHAPTER 13

'A man always has
hopes when he is free'

EDWARD CLIFFORD, a railroad detective, patrolled Weehawken on the New Jersey shoreline, across the Hudson
River from New York City. In the early hours of the morning on
the day after Frank Davis was caught he spotted a fire near the
riverside railroad tracks. They were close to the palisades and
cliffside where tramps often sheltered, so he decided to check
them out. As he approached, he saw a group of men huddled over
the fire and one standing alone, further away. The man's face was
covered in dirt, but Clifford was suspicious. He walked away and
called a police officer.

When Oliver Perry spotted the officer, he scrambled up the cliff
to a narrow path on a ledge in the rock. He got about a hundred
yards along it before losing his footing and falling on to the rocks
below. His ankle badly sprained, he could barely walk and within
minutes he was pinned to the ground.

Perry limped painfully as they walked him to the police station
in Weehawken and reportedly begged, 'I'll do anything for you.
I'll cut wood or do any honest work. Don't send me back there
again.' But in custody, questioned by the Chief of Police, Simon
Kelly, he insisted that he was a labourer who had fallen on hard

times and did not want his family to know he was destitute. He was, in short, just one of the many tramps who hung around the industrial shoreline of the Hudson. He certainly looked the part. He was wearing a short black sack coat tucked into worn, torn trousers, held up by suspenders worn over the jacket, a battered hat and shoes split along the sides. In the pocket of the coat was an old newspaper but not a single cent.

If Perry's outfit resembled a parody of Dickens's Artful Dodger, his physical condition was no laughing matter. His face was pinched and weather-beaten and he had clearly had little to eat for some time. And when his shoes were removed, it was clear that the fall from the cliff was not the only reason for his halting gait. His feet were so badly swollen, blistered and cut that it was surprising he had managed to walk at all. They also seemed to have been badly burnt by lime, almost certainly from walking barefoot in brickyards near Matteawan.

His pathetic condition appeared to arouse Chief Kelly's sympathy. It is possible, of course, that the policeman was using his head rather than being all heart, hoping to gain his prisoner's trust. Whatever prompted him, he treated his prisoner with kindness. He sent out for breakfast, which Perry ate ravenously, and had his feet bathed and bandaged. But if Perry was exhausted and battered, he seemed, remarkably, to be displaying all his old coolness under pressure. When he was free he displayed an ability to make the best of even a bad situation as consistently as in prison he made it worse. As he had in Lyons, he initially resisted admitting his identity, but eventually, after a detective from the Mulberry Street police headquarters in New York City had arrived with a photograph, he called for Kelly and offered to give him a full confession.

Once again, Perry tried to take charge of the situation, rather than waiting to be pushed. It seems that he also had no illusions about Kelly's possible motives. The man who had once calculated the value of his own image knew exactly what rewards his reflected celebrity could bestow on someone else.

Kelly, who would soon become Mayor of Weehawken, wasted no time in displaying his famous prisoner. Outside, word of his capture had spread and hordes of people were arriving in the small town. Among them were reporters who had raced up from New York City, eager to get an interview and ready to reward the man who gave it and the man who allowed it. As soon as Perry's questioning ended, he was given a chair in the jail corridor and the waiting reporters were admitted. They had come prepared, remembering his taste for cigars as well as for attention. It was his first interview for three years.

Perry seemed relaxed, almost his old self, sometimes laughing as he recalled particular events, sometimes becoming more thoughtful, stroking his bruised feet and staring into the distance. The listening reporters, who had warned the public about this ruthless man's violent tendencies and claimed he would not be captured alive, waxed lyrical about his clear, frank gaze and fluent conversation. The interview itself, however, was not an entirely sedate exercise. Every few minutes policemen, brandishing clubs, rushed outside to drive crowds away from the windows where they were climbing on to one another's shoulders to catch a glimpse of Perry.

Inside, Perry described his first night on the run. 'I followed the east star. The moon rose early. But the moon travelled so fast that to follow it one goes around in a circle. I selected that star because I know it is a fixed star.' He had not lost his knack of appealing to the press as one positively rhapsodic account of his journey revealed: 'This man of crime went forth under the stars, with the soft light of the moon bathing him in its splendour. . . . What thoughts, what fancies spread through his distorted mind no one knows.' The romantic vision of the vulnerable man blessed by the lights of heaven was not cluttered by facts. After giving them his best image, Perry flatly refused to provide any information about his first few days on the run, although he insisted, almost in tears, that he had not stolen anything and was ashamed of the way he looked in his ragged clothes.

He eventually said that he had made his way to New York City, refusing to say where he had stayed. Instead he told a long story of how he had been repeatedly turned away from charitable hospitals before eventually being given perfunctory treatment for his wounded feet. 'If I have a mania,' he commented, 'it is the exposing of the cruel manner in which unfortunates are treated in public institutions.' The statement was undoubtedly heartfelt but he would also, conveniently, strike a chord with the liberal New Yorkers who were beginning to protest about the treatment of the poor and needy and who might, in turn, be sympathetic to his own cause. It was the first hint that Perry might say something controversial about his experiences in the asylum or in prison.

He gave only a vague account of how he ended up on the Weehawken shoreline, and no reason for heading there, but hinted that he had been helped by a number of women who took pity on a stranger down on his luck. The Perry charm had clearly not deserted him even if his condition was less than glamorous. But for all his bravado, and whatever spin he might put on it after the event, his time on the run was not easy. Freedom meant everything to Perry, but it came at a price.

Touchingly, he seems to have been caught because he craved not only the warmth of the tramps' fire, but also their company; 'I was cold and the fire looked bright and cheerful. The company of the tramps, too, was not unwelcome, for I was lonesome.'

The man who had admitted to being lonely also seemed, underneath the swagger and wit, to be preoccupied and even rather frightened. When someone suggested he would have been caught eventually anyway, he replied thoughtfully, 'A man always has hopes when he is free, and I had a heavy, long sentence before me.' Then, *The World*'s man observed, 'this man of nerve paused, and his grey eyes seemed to be looking far away. They are fascinating eyes, that suggest sinister things.' Perry was clearly worried about returning to the asylum but, with characteristic bravado, issued a warning: 'If they abuse me as they have in the past I'll take any means to attract the attention of the world to myself. God knows I've suffered enough there already. I'm an American, and, although a criminal, I'm not a bad man.'

When Dr Lamb arrived to collect Perry, he was shocked to find that his patient had gone. He had been taken to the more secure Hudson County Jail in Jersey City to wait for requisition papers. Because Perry had crossed the state line between New York and New Jersey, extradition papers signed by the Governor of New York and countersigned by the Governor of New Jersey were needed before he could be sent back to Matteawan. Perry's threatened showdown with the asylum authorities might be delayed.

CHAPTER 14

Habeas Corpus

The World's illustration of Perry,
Clifford and Kelly after his capture
(Reproduced from the collection
of the Library of Congress).

PERRY DID not wait to be taken back to Matteawan before speaking out about the abuse he claimed to have suffered there. He spent a night sharing a cell on Murderers' Row with Paul Genz, a man who had killed his wife and was convinced he deserved to die. Determined not to be sent back to Matteawan without a fight, Perry used an interview with some of the most influential reporters in the state to launch a campaign against the asylum's regime. Bathed, shaved and rested, he sat outside the cell with his now customary cigar. His manner as he described his experiences impressed his audience, and the *New York Times* spoke for all the press when it noted that 'there was nothing in his appearance, manner, or conversation to indicate insanity'.

Perry's account of Matteawan made, and makes, disturbing reading. He described two methods of punishment used when men were unruly, often when keepers deliberately provoked a patient into 'giving a cross word, and then they begin'. The first was a brutal assault: 'One keeper will grasp a man's neck from behind, and, after the fashion of a garrotter, will compress his windpipe and shut off the air from his lungs. He is then thrown to the ground and held there by two men, while others kick him in the stomach and side with the side of their boots. This style of kicking is used so as not to leave marks and is called "hoofing". The blood gushes from the patient's mouth until he becomes insensible, and is carried to a room, where he lies for hours before recovering consciousness.' While these beatings generally took place at night and were inflicted illicitly by the keepers, the second form of punishment was administered by the physicians, as part of the legal 'treatment' of patients: 'The other punishment is the "black medicine", which as I understand, is a decoction of opiates. It makes the patient's mind active, so that he has delusions, but paralyses the body so that he cannot move. The effect lasts five or six hours, and sometimes three doses a day are given.'

He described the process of being drugged. 'I suppose I became excited, for the doctor said I had a delusion. After I had talked to Dr Lamb, four keepers . . . threw themselves upon me and knocked me down. While these men held me Dr Lamb injected some drug into my arm, and I became unconscious. When I recovered my senses the next day I was lying completely nude on the floor of my cell. I complained to Dr Daly about being drugged. I said I wanted exercise or work, anything to keep me occupied, and from brooding over my condition.' The drugs brought unconsciousness but also hallucinations, sometimes of terrifying creatures, sometimes, as Perry recalled with bitter humour, of more mundane things, as in an incident when the floor tiles seemed to turn into pieces of pie, his favourite dessert. Visions apart, his distrust of institutional food was exacerbated by his discovery that drugs were routinely added to it. Although he did not know whether this was on the orders of the medical staff, or was a practice adopted by the keepers to make their job easier, he had experienced similar symptoms after eating to those caused by injections.

He may have escaped from Matteawan because, having recovered from his breakdown, he was gripped by the compulsive need to get away. But, having been caught, he now started to campaign against the regime he had complained about to Amelia Haswell. Once again he demonstrated his remarkable ability to appeal to particular audiences. Just as he had worked the press and public in Lyons by constructing a romantic image of himself, so now he seemed to target sections of the press and the public who were already calling for reform of penal institutions. While his protests were undoubtedly heartfelt, he also began to use reformers' terminology and references to suit his own ends and turned every interview to the subject of this new campaign.

While some of the behaviour of both attendants and physicians may have been occasioned by the frustrations of dealing with the violently insane, some was undoubtedly the result of a relative indifference to their rights, as a growing number of New Yorkers had begun to argue. Asylums, like prisons, were closed worlds where brutality and cruelty could go unnoticed and complaints by the victims unheard. Unusually, Perry, who had every reason to be both angry and intemperate, and was still officially classed as insane, offered a rational explanation for the regime. Middle-class reformers regularly condemned the prison workers who abused patients, seeing them as brutes, almost sub-human, without attempting to examine their place in an exploitative system that showed them as little respect as they afforded their charges. Perry was no friend of guards or keepers, but he did understand the economic problem. The attendants were, he said, 'brutal, ignorant fellows' but they were 'hired at $20 a month'. How, he asked, could intelligent men be expected to apply for such posts? Perry was ambitious in his target: he wanted to attack the whole regime, not just the workers.

The press divided sharply over Perry's new role as a protestor. While he was always good copy, most newspapers followed clear party-political lines on issues like institutional reform. In an intriguing contrast to his days in Lyons, when his treatment by the Republican sheriff had been attacked by the Democrat press, now it was the latter that called for Perry's allegations to be investigated, and the Republican press that dismissed them. He won some serious supporters from the respectable press. Although his paper included a far from flattering phrenologist's 'reading' of Perry's head, the editor of the *New York Times* took his new stance seriously. He reserved judgment on Perry's specific claims, but called for an investigation solely on the basis that Perry was evidently sane.

Henry Allison refuted Perry's charges, insisting that attendants were never permitted to use unnecessary force, except in self-defence. Perry, he claimed, was 'subject to uncontrollable maniacal excitement, during which he is extremely noisy and defiant, so that he disturbs the whole ward, refuses to listen to reason, and is extremely threatening in language and manner . . .' He also denied that the ability of Perry and his companions' to plot the escape was proof of sanity: 'It is a trade with them, the same as the carpenter's trade or any other trade a man learns. They are criminals and it is their business to conspire.'

Inside the jail, Perry was proving very popular with his fellow prisoners, including the depressed Genz, who surprised everyone by washing and bandaging his new cellmate's feet. He and other inmates, including Thomas McLaren, who had murdered his mistress, and George Armstrong, a wealthy 'green-goods' man or confidence trickster, almost came to blows as they tried to outdo one another and the guards in looking after their famous companion. But while Perry enjoyed the attention, he seemed increasingly agitated. Repeatedly advised to sit so that his feet might heal, he kept standing up, as if unable to stay still. Bystanders noticed him pulling his weight off his feet by grasping the bars of the cell tightly behind him.

Although he was no longer in the grip of a debilitating breakdown, his behaviour suggests that he was still in a fragile condition, distressed by confinement and increasingly anxious about being sent back to an asylum whose keepers and doctors he had publicly denounced. He admitted to his cellmates that he was worried about retribution, and said that, if only he had the hidden fortune he was rumoured to have, he would do anything, pay anyone, even to delay his return. Given a chance, he told them, he would fight for his liberty 'inch by inch'.

Meanwhile, the battle over the reward for his capture had intensified. Chief Kelly called on Governor George Werts of New Jersey, on the day after Perry's arrival in Jersey City, to ask him not to endorse the requisition papers until the reward had been paid to the Weehawken detective and policeman whose claims were being challenged by the former's boss. Werts agreed. Then a second man asked for a delay. But Alexander Simpson, a local lawyer, was not acting on behalf of any of the reward chasers. George Armstrong, the 'green-goods' man, had hired him to work for Perry. It seems an extraordinary act of generosity. Perhaps Perry had hinted that he could pay him back, perhaps Armstrong, like Kelly, hoped to make something from his association with the star criminal, or perhaps he just liked him.

The following day Perry was to appear in court, but there was a problem. His feet were so painful that he said he was unable to walk the 200 feet from the jail to the courthouse. So, followed by a large crowd, an under-sheriff and a constable made a basket of their hands and, with his arms around their necks, carried him to the courthouse, up two flights of stairs and into the hearing. It made a striking scene, emphasizing Perry's broken condition. Simpson immediately asked for a writ of habeas corpus. He had decided to challenge Perry's identification by exploiting the vagueness of the commitment papers. Justice Lippincott, following the letter of the law, agreed and ordered that Perry be held until proper evidence of his identity had been produced. While the move was exploiting a legal technicality, it offered Perry some hope of delaying his return to Matteawan and a chance to air his grievances in open court.

Henry Allison, who had assumed he would be taking Perry back to Matteawan, issued a statement to waiting reporters, insisting that Perry was both insane and 'untrustworthy', and went home. His mood can hardly have been improved by the atmosphere in the jail, where Perry was being treated like a hero.

Like so many celebrities today, Perry had even been commissioned by a newspaper to write his own story. *The World* printed his own version of his life and crimes, complete with a reproduction of his signature. Sub-headings provided a safe moral framework for the sensational story but the appeal was clearly the 'voice' of the star.

'I do not consider myself a great criminal or a cold-blooded desperado. Many a man who sits in his office in Wall Street is as much a robber as I am. It is simply a difference in methods . . . I had no ambition to be a dime-novel hero. . . . I did not want this notoriety. I am not proud of it.' He reiterated his allegations of institutional corruption and brutality and defended his friends, Frank Davis, 'a man who had forgotten more than I ever knew', and Amelia Haswell: 'She has been like a mother to me . . . They said she was something more to me than that, and tried to bring scandal on her good name . . . and I have been driven almost wild, knowing I was powerless to protect her and that she suffered through her friendship to me.'

Whatever his feelings for the missionary, he revealed that he could no longer claim to be a believer. 'I have received letters from religious friends, exhorting me to turn from evil and serve God in prison. I may disappoint them, because I can't see things quite as they do. Their religion is enough for their lives but I have had other experiences. I am not a fanatic like some. I can't believe everything I read in the Bible, nor that I have heard in churches. I do believe in the religion of doing right, however far I have been from living up to it.' Those who thought his religiosity was a clever ploy to manipulate gullible do-gooders must have been taken aback. Even a teller of tall tales may speak the truth. If Perry had rejected Christianity, he had clearly not replaced it, as

Amelia Haswell had feared, with a radical political creed, although he did joke, 'I do not know anything about Socialism or Anarchism, but I know that when a man takes it on himself to equalize unjustly distributed wealth by robbing express trains, he makes a mistake.'

He gave brief stories of both his train robberies, then turned to his own character. 'I realize that society will not tolerate men of the stamp I proved myself. I realize that when a man once steps outside the law, every hand is raised against him, and he is hunted down like a wild beast.' But, he continued, 'I don't think I have vicious instincts. I'm not any better than I might be and during my imprisonment I have been so brutalized by association with the most degraded men; I have been so knocked about, sworn at, drugged and beaten that I have lost, perhaps, a good share of what refinement I ever had.

'The newspapers have called me a "gentleman desperado" and have spoken of my hands and slender fingers, the hands of a man who has never done hard work. Right here I want to correct that. I am an uneducated country boy. I grew up without schooling. Whatever I have learned I have learned by experience . . .'

But if he was proud of his humble origins, he was also keen to show that he had good taste, even if it differed from that shown by those who followed his adventures so avidly. 'I enjoy a good book and I like to read American history. I never had any taste for sensational literature, dime novels and detective stories, even as a boy.' He complained that all he could get hold of at Matteawan were 'Irish newspapers of Nationalist proclivities', and expressed a particular liking for the works of Nathaniel Hawthorne. He claimed that his favourite was, appropriately enough, *The House of the Seven Gables*, which tells the story of a man released from a

long and unjust prison sentence. He also revealed that the diary
he kept in Lyons had been just the start of a writing habit that was
becoming a passion. 'I used to spend some of my long nights of
sleeplessness during my imprisonment making rhymes. I'm nothing of a poet, but I can jingle words, and in the long night watches
it helped to pass the time when I could not sleep.'

Books duly started arriving at the jail for Perry, along with
flowers, cigars, boxes of fruit and candies, sent or brought by
well-wishers. 'Why, what a nice little fellow,' said one female
visitor, 'he doesn't look bloodthirsty at all, does he?' Recovering
from the indignities of dressing as a tramp, he regained his old
sartorial style when a local clothier delivered a new suit to the jail.
Perry promptly sent a note back, which the clothier published in
the local newspapers. It read: 'Kind Sir, If clothes make the man
and gentleman, then I am sure, for I feel more respectful [sic] since
receiving your kind gift. May the success that follows all just men
be with you. Yours, O.C. Perry. N.B. Please excuse the chiro-
graphy, for the drugs have caused it.' In fact the $15 suit had been
paid for by Chief Kelly, but the clothier saw his opportunity for
some free publicity, while Perry evidently saw a chance to remind
the public in his carefully worded postscript of the effects of the
'black medicine'.

This mutually beneficial relationship continued when Perry,
clearly still aware of his 'market value', offered the clothier a deal.
In return for a set of underclothes and a shirt he would sit for a
photograph that the shopkeeper could use in future publicity.
Astonishingly, the Sheriff did not object. Perry asked for three or
four dozen copies of the picture, hoping to sell them as souvenirs
to the men and women who visited the jail to see him. His fame
was soon confirmed by a visit, staged by a newspaper, of one of

ica's other most notorious criminals, George Bidwell, who, twenty-five years earlier, had stolen nearly $5 million from the Bank of England.

Perry's evident enjoyment of his renewed celebrity gradually began to worry even those editors who took his allegations of abuses at Matteawan seriously. His rather too adept manipulation of public feeling through the press was beginning to make him a less attractive figure to those who had sympathized with his situation. And the legal battles to keep him out of Matteawan were beginning to have a farcical aspect that threatened to make not only the asylum authorities but also the law look foolish.

Was Perry undermining his own case by enjoying his brief spell of pleasure and control too much? Could his desire for attention, admiration and the brief pleasures of winning a battle of wits be as compulsive as his need to escape? While the liberal press still called for an investigation, the conservative press bristled at his easy life in jail, condemning the 'rising tide of swash' caused by his 'hair-raising tales of Torquemada-like atrocities' and mocking his protestor's credentials as well as his popularity: 'if the people admire his type of citizenship, let him be canonized, pardoned by the Governor and sent to the State Senate as a Lexow Reformer'. Lexow had produced a shocking report on police corruption that was clearly not to the editor's liking. Even he stopped short of recommending one exasperated editor's solution to the problem of Perry: execution.

Ironically, it was Henry Allison who gave the liberal press the ammunition they needed to renew their attacks on the state's penal institutions through Perry's allegations. If he hoped to quash Perry's claims, he was badly misguided. He gave a detailed description of the use of drugs in Matteawan that merely supported Perry's case. He admitted that the drug hyoscin, with which Perry had been treated four or five times, caused drying of the body's mucous membranes and the tongue, and impaired vision, but said these side effects were easily counteracted by stimulants and caused no long-term damage. One reporter challenged Allison to say what the effects would have been on a man who 'was already thirsty and sane', arguing that such drugs should not be part of 'the modern enlightened method of treating insane patients'.

Dr Carlos MacDonald, President of the State Lunacy Commission, swiftly issued a vehement defence of the system, Matteawan and its Superintendent. His assessment of Perry was clear: 'Perry is a type of lunatic that is found in all criminal asylums in which desperate and criminal tendencies are interwoven with insanity. Such persons also have a morbid love of notoriety and enjoy immensely being the central figure of a public sensation or scandal. Such persons usually excite the sympathies of the morbid curiosity seekers who, actuated by maudlin sentiment, visit prisons and jails and bestow attention upon notorious criminals.' Those who agreed had ready evidence of Perry's impact on at least one such person. After the hearing he was visited by Amelia Haswell. 'There goes my best friend in the east,' he said as she left.

The legal process of extraditing Perry seemed to be spinning out almost indefinitely, much to his relief and the pleasure of the hotel and saloon keepers who were catering to the press. Writs and warrants piled up until eventually, after a week, Governor Werts stepped in and signed the requisition papers without waiting for Justice Lippincott's judgment. Relations between neighbouring states had to be protected. Lippincott tried to muster as much dignity as he could and announced that Perry would have his day in court.

When it came, the courtroom was crowded as everyone waited for the final act in the legal drama. Perry's lawyer made one last attempt to stop the extradition, insisting that as only sane men could testify in court, and as Perry could not be denied a hearing before being extradited, he would have to stay in New Jersey until he was either proved to be sane or had regained his sanity. But Lippincott was firm, in decision if not tone. 'I do not see, in view of the evidence, that I can do anything but refuse the defendant the discharge asked for, and order that he be remanded to the custody of the sheriff to await action on the requisition from the governor of New York.' The battle was over.

Perry was taken from the court, handcuffed to a keeper and still walking with difficulty. He was to be accompanied back to Matteawan by Dr Lamb and Chief Kelly. Suddenly, to everyone's amazement, he turned to his lawyer, swore and slapped him across the face. Perry was pulled away and the party moved on. Simpson said nothing. Instead he ran to the Justice's office to demand that a warrant be issued against Perry for assault and battery. Two police constables were given the warrant and set off to arrest and detain Perry. Perry had not lashed out in anger but was enacting a scripted final scene in the legal farce. He had been told by his lawyer to hit him so that he could be arrested and kept in New Jersey while new legal manoeuvres were planned.

But Dr Lamb was too fast this time. He quickly signed the receipt for his prisoner, had him bundled into a waiting coach and set off for the railroad station. Before the police could catch up to arrest Perry, the party had boarded the train and headed for New York.

It is not difficult to imagine what Perry must have felt as he returned to face the men he had accused of brutality. In Jersey City the public excitement about his case and the attention of press and sympathizers had once more kept some of his fears of being incarcerated at bay. Now the reality was all too apparent. But when the train pulled in to Fishkill landing he made a good show, handing out his photographs to the waiting crowd. Henry Allison announced that Perry would be placed in one of the general wards and would not be returned to solitary confinement unless his behaviour made it necessary.

He may privately have wondered how long it would be before Perry or one of his keepers forced another confrontation. But in June, two months after the arrest that had convinced so many that Perry was sane, Allison announced that he was sending him back to Auburn, 'free from any active mental disturbance'. The announcement sat rather oddly with Dr MacDonald's earlier confident assessment of Perry's lunacy but to those who had been impressed by Perry it was good news. His fellow fugitives had mixed fortunes. Frank Davis attempted suicide by hanging himself with a sheet and faced a lifetime in Matteawan. Patrick Maguire plotted another escape, before betraying the keeper who was helping him and earning a return to Sing-Sing to complete the four years of his sentence. John Quigley disappeared from public record.

On 2 July 1895 Perry made the long journey back to Auburn, this time overnight. He arrived at half past eight in the morning and was met by reporters who noted he was heavier than he had been before his transfer to Matteawan, but looked haggard and careworn. As he walked from the train he told reporters, 'I can see where I have erred in my life, and if I get my liberty again I will lead an honest life.' He insisted publicly that he was glad to return to Auburn, conforming to his usual pattern of trying to win sympathy. Bizarrely, given his earlier paranoia about being poisoned, he even compared the prison rations favourably with those in Matteawan. But he also declared that he had no intention of working without pay. Although he maintained a cool front, his fear of retribution by keepers was soon revealed when he privately begged the Warden for a transfer to Clinton, the prison whose reputation was so tough it had deterred him in 1891 from giving himself up.

The Warden insisted that if he conducted himself properly, he would receive fair treatment. Then he was returned to his old cell in the basement. It was reported that he would not be made to work. He might have recovered from his last breakdown, but now the conditions, dictated by the authorities and self-imposed, for mental collapse were once more in place.

CHAPTER 15

A Missionary's Work

WHILE PERRY faced life in Auburn, the investigations into his escape from Matteawan took a sensational turn. Two suspected accomplices were identified. One, predictably, was a keeper. The other was the respectable Troy City missionary, Amelia Haswell.

Amelia Haswell was the daughter of an English naval captain who moved to New York State to raise his family on a farm. She was born in 1849 and dedicated her whole life to God and those Americans who had little reason to count their blessings. Living as a single woman in an industrial city, she learned first-hand about the sufferings of ordinary Americans. As well as serving as the Troy City missionary, she supported the Women's Temperance Union, campaigning to end the social evils of drink, and the Fresh Air Fund, a charity that arranged country excursions for poor urban children. She also worked for the less obviously deserving, including prisoners and prostitutes, regularly visiting them in jail and speaking for them in court. She was on vacation in Ocean Grove, a New Jersey seaside resort run on Christian principles as a permanent camp meeting, when it was reported that her arrest was imminent and a lengthy prison sentence likely.

A former keeper at Matteawan, William E. Hopkins, accused of helping Perry in his April escape, had confessed and implicated her in the crime.

Newspapers were filled with speculation about her conduct and character. Acts that had once won her the respect of fellow Christians and, at worst, the mild scorn of sceptics, were now condemned as reckless or even corrupt. The police claimed that if any criminal convinced Amelia Haswell of his or her desire to lead a better life, she would help them avoid arrest by whatever means she could, in defiance of the law. Her relationship with Perry was described as 'mysterious', and the age difference between them became a constant theme in reports that bordered on character assassination. Although he clearly saw her as a 'Mother', detectives and reporters repeatedly insinuated that she was romantically infatuated with him. The sweeping criticism extended to her 'not very prepossessing' appearance. She was described as 'taller than the average woman, inclined to stoop', with 'a sallow complexion', and as being obliged 'to wear glasses'. The *Sun* struggled to be more positive: 'She is an intellectual looking woman, but would hardly be considered handsome.' Whatever her answer to possible criminal charges, Amelia Haswell had already been found guilty of being less than a perfect model of femininity.

In truth, she was undoubtedly naïve and unworldly in her dealings with Perry and the other troubled or damaged men and women she tried to help. She was a woman of unshakable faith and utterly binding principles who was prepared to battle with authority and bend man's law if it conflicted with her totally sincere interpretation of God's. She was formidable as a foe, as the Pinkertons had discovered, and, as Perry knew and sometimes exploited, ever faithful as a friend. She was not in love with Perry in the simple sense implied by those who sniggered, but she certainly loved him. She was undoubtedly taken in at times, too easily convinced by his romantic stories, too keen to see the best in him, but she was no fool. When she indulged Oliver Perry, it was a mother's indulgence of a wayward son. He may not always have been sincere when he called her Mother and listened to her advice, but Amelia Haswell took her motherly duties seriously.

Amelia Haswell's interest in Perry was clearly prompted by her Christian faith and social conscience, but there was definitely a more personal bond between them. They were worlds apart in background, age and general temperament. Yet, like Perry, she was passionate, eloquent and impetuous. She may have been a little infatuated with the charismatic, damaged young man who walked into her class, but she may also have recognized something of herself in him. Was she drawn to the young robber because he reminded her of a part of herself? Be that as it may, her impetuosity and unworldliness eventually landed her in serious trouble.

William Hopkins had been arrested when detectives working for American Express had uncovered a second escape plot by Perry while still at Matteawan. He had apparently bribed a keeper to help him and confided in him that Hopkins had provided the keys that had been used in the earlier escape. The keeper informed Allison, Perry was held in solitary confinement until he was sent to Auburn and Hopkins was arrested.

Hopkins was in his forties, with a wife and children and a serious drinking problem. Confronted with the evidence against him he admitted his guilt and, after some prompting, implicated

Amelia Haswell. He said that in the fall of 1894 she had sent him a parcel of jewellery that Perry was giving him as a reward for his help in his planned escape, which included providing the keys, a file and blank keys and unlocking the cell of Maguire, whom Perry had brought into the plan because he was a skilled jeweller. Hopkins also confessed to telling Perry he would leave clothes and a pistol at an agreed spot near a local racetrack, but that instead he had got roaring drunk in the village. His testimony revealed that Perry had planned his escape even more carefully than had been thought. It also suggested that he had a rather respectable accomplice. According to the Matteawan authorities, Haswell had visited Perry regularly, bringing him religious reading matter. The prisoner had, they said, spoken often of the spiritual solace she brought him. Now they suspected that her support had been more practical.

Hopkins had already sold the jewellery, which he thought was from Perry's haul in his first train robbery, so detectives were sent to search jewellers and pawn shops. Soon a watch, two rings, one set with a two-carat diamond, the other a 'beauty' with a fourteen-carat diamond, were returned to American Express. What was Amelia Haswell doing with these in the first place, let alone sending them to a keeper as a bribe?

There is no record of exactly what, or how, Perry was told about what was happening to his 'Mother', but his own circumstances had taken a turn for the worse. Still driven by his compulsion to escape, made worse if anything by his glimpses of the world, he was discovered smuggling sand from the exercise yard. He had been filling his pockets when the guards were not looking, and storing it in his cell to make a sand bag to use as a weapon. When it was found in a surprise inspection, he was once more placed in the dungeon. On release he was held in solitary confinement in his gloomy cell in the basement corridor, now occupied by condemned men for whom there were no death cells. He was the only prisoner in his row who had not been sentenced to death.

While Amelia Haswell stayed in Ocean Grove, no move was made to arrest her because this would have required extradition proceedings that would have revealed prosecution evidence. As soon as she returned to Troy she would be arrested. Understandably, she did not hurry and Ocean Grove's religious services, with congregations of over seven thousand, gave her plenty of spiritual succour. Meanwhile, her friends and associates proclaimed her good character and innocence of any charges that might be made against her. They claimed that, far from breaking the law, she was an honest woman who had been hounded by detectives and the 'old Troy police ring', a byword for political corruption.

She remained silent until the enterprising editor of the *Troy Times* telegraphed her at the gloriously named Ocean Queen Hotel to invite her to tell her story. To everyone's surprise, she replied with a letter that was immediately published across the state. In it she acknowledged that she had indeed sent jewellery to Hopkins at Perry's request, but insisted that it was an innocent act. The jewellery, she said, was not stolen but Perry's legal property. Perry had originally asked her to sell his watch because it 'would be old-fashioned, and he would realize more for it now than a few years hence'. Perry also asked her to sell two rings, sent to her after his trial by the Wayne County sheriff. Whether or not what Perry said about the jewellery was true, Amelia may easily, if a little naïvely, have believed that it was not stolen. She had expressed some reluctance after her past experiences, so Perry suggested she send them to a 'friend' called Hopkins who would sell them. He made no reference to Hopkins being a keeper. 'I enquired', she wrote, 'whether he felt sure he could trust this man. I explained that so many would take advantage of his help-lessness.' Perry replied, 'If ever I had a friend this man is one. He feels sorry for me, and would not betray me.'

Haswell eventually agreed and sent the parcel, covering her tracks – almost certainly unwittingly – by letting a friend post it for her. The next she heard of it was weeks after the escape, when Perry, back in Matteawan, wrote asking her to visit him. She did so, with her aunt, and he told her the truth about his deal with Hopkins, complaining that Hopkins had let him down. Instead of telling the police, or even the asylum authorities, Amelia Haswell wrote to Hopkins asking him to return the jewellery and, when he was obstructive, to Perry's father, telling him about what Hopkins had done so that he could demand his son's property. She was, she wrote, 'indignant to think a keeper would encourage Oliver in wrongdoing', but her desire to protect Perry from further punishment and, possibly, understandable reluctance at being implicated herself, restrained her from following the proper course of action according to the law.

She offered no apologies about her conduct and insisted that in her relationship with Perry 'God knows there is nothing I am ashamed to proclaim from the housetops.' She even claimed that the charge that she had knowingly helped Perry escape was an act of revenge by detectives whom she had defied since 1891: 'All through the period following the robbery, and after the arrest, the detectives kept up their persecution of me. I knew at different times where Perry was in hiding, but I did not choose to betray him. They used all their persuasions, arguments and threats. But his life was in my hands, and I would not give him up.'

If her accusation was contentious, others were even more dramatic. Rumours spread that the campaign against her was being orchestrated by influential men, including Thomas C. Platt. 'Boss' Platt, known as 'The Machiavelli of Tioga County', was a powerful Republican with a reputation for tough, some said corrupt, dealings and a known dislike of reformers like Amelia Haswell. No conspiracy was ever proved but supporters of big business may well have been impatient with the meddling missionary. It was reported that over the past year American Express had lost about $200,000 in robberies and the company was more jealous than ever of its property and reputation.

Damaging rumours proliferated about Amelia Haswell, ranging from complicity in planning the first robbery to hiding the saw in Perry's Bible. But the consequences of being found guilty of the current charges were serious enough. American Express was considering pressing charges for handling stolen goods, the United States Mail could charge her with using the mails for improper purposes, and the District Attorney of Dutchess County, as a representative of the State of New York, could prosecute her for aiding the escape of a felon. While all the possible charges were serious, the latter was a felony for which her sentence, if convicted, would match Perry's: forty-nine years.

The scene was set for a dramatic trial. Amelia Haswell was peacefully arrested when she returned home and, accompanied by her aunt and her brother-in-law, the Reverend John Warren, she was waved off on the railroad journey to the hearing in Poughkeepsie by a large crowd of Christians and reformers. The hearing, to determine if there was enough evidence to hold her for a Grand Jury trial, was so overcrowded that it had to move to a bigger courtroom. Amelia Haswell entered a plea of not guilty. From the start her flamboyant lawyer, Calvin Keach, set his tone by reading the names of all the influential citizens who had offered to stand bail for his client, clearly hoping to establish her good reputation in contrast to the drunken chief witness.

Henry Allison's testimony offered no first-hand evidence of Haswell's complicity in Perry's escape, although he insisted that she had conversations with Perry that could not be overheard. It was clear that the missionary had complained on numerous occasions about Perry's treatment and especially about drunken keepers but, although Allison admitted that he had subsequently sacked one of them, he thought she was generally misguided. Eyebrows were raised when he claimed, 'She told me that Perry had never done anything for which he should be severely punished. He had only robbed an express company, she said, and did not appear to consider that a serious matter.'

Hopkins repeated his allegations and insisted that she had known he was a keeper and written to him as such. He also said that she had advised him not to keep the distinctive watch in case it was recognized.

His evidence might turn out to be untrue, and his reward of immunity from prosecution might have made some suspicious of his motives, but it was unsettling for Haswell's supporters. Keach announced that his client wished to make a personal statement but he needed an adjournment to prepare and to subpoena several witnesses. The case was adjourned for one week and Amelia Haswell put up bail of $1,000, signed for by her aunt and her lawyer.

Reactions to the hearing were typified by Judge Robertson of

Troy. He spoke in defence of Amelia Haswell, praising her good work and intentions, but he clearly had reservations. 'You know Perry was a remarkable criminal, exceptionally bright, and the kind of man that many people pitied, believing he could be saved . . . Miss Haswell took a great deal of interest in his case. Some people may think it possible that her zeal made her indiscreet in some respects . . .'

Amelia Haswell was accompanied to the reconvened hearing by a number of well-known religious and political figures, including the candidate for State Treasurer on the prohibition ticket. The forces of reform and redemption were displaying their support. Keach opened the proceedings by reading her lengthy statement. She denied any involvement in Perry's escape, and explained that she had not gone to the police when she discovered what had happened because she did not want to punish Hopkins's innocent family. Even when her actions were legally suspect, she was anxious to explain, sounding rather like Perry himself, that her moral motives were sound.

At the core of her statement, and of her recent attitude towards Perry, was her obvious sense of responsibility, even guilt, for the heavy sentence he was serving. Having personally persuaded him to plead guilty at his trial, believing according to her Christian principles that it might lead to clemency, she had been deeply shocked at the severity of his sentence. Now, defensively, she stressed that she had done her duty and suffered persecution as a result. 'I firmly believe', she argued, 'that if I had not done voluntarily all that I could to detect and convict Oliver Curtis Perry of that crime, he never would have been convicted.' For her pains she had been hounded by detectives who had made threats 'that they would never rest until they got me in prison'.

She closed by touching on what interested many people most of all. 'It has been commented on much in public prints and private gossip, that I felt a deep interest in Mr Perry. I confess I have and still do, as is common with my lifework in the field of trying to reform the wicked of the earth. There is no sentimental false sympathy in my heart toward this man or any other. . . . What is the mission of a missionary unless it be to raise the fallen and stop others from falling?'

At the end of her statement affidavits were read and witnesses, including Haswell's aunt, were called to support her story. Finally William Hopkins took the stand. He had arrived late, and his replies to questions were often non-committal or confused, giving the impression that he had been schooled by the detectives but had forgotten his lines.

Keach moved that his client be released as there was 'not one scintilla of evidence to show her guilt' and a heated exchange began about whether Perry as a thief or Hopkins as a law-breaking keeper was less reliable. Finally the Recorder inter-vened. In his apparent anxiety to conclude the hearing without assuming any responsibility, he sounded like a latter-day Pontius Pilate. 'Although I might discharge this defendant, the District Attorney would still, of course, have the right to present the case for indictment . . . I will not bear any of the burden and will hold the defendant to await the grand jury's action.' Amelia Haswell was granted bail at $2,000, paid by her aunt. To the waiting press she spoke only briefly: 'So much of it is over. I shall continue to place my trust in God.'

The Grand Jury met at the beginning of October and was as decisive in judgment as the Recorder had been hesitant. Amelia Haswell's months of anxiety were swiftly ended as the jury found no grounds for indictment and the case was dismissed. While there would still be whispers about the propriety of her relationship with Perry, the missionary had convinced at least some of the public that she was no felon. Predictably, the dismissal was barely reported by the newspapers that had splashed the accusations across their pages. Amelia Haswell herself felt totally vindicated and declared her intention to continue the work that had led her to court. A few days later, the *Troy Times* published her own lengthy account of her trials, entitled 'A Pure Heart's Triumph', which concluded: 'I have never had such sympathy for the poor and oppressed and erring as I have today, and I can assure the world at large, as far as is in my power, they will have a warmer friend than ever before in Amelia E. Haswell.'

CHAPTER 16

'Oblivion where he belongs'

O N 17 SEPTEMBER, while Amelia Haswell was waiting for the Grand Jury hearing that would clear her name, an extraordinary and terrible event in Auburn transformed Oliver Perry's life. Late in the evening a keeper heard a moaning noise in his cell and went to investigate. When he peered through the door he saw Perry holding a piece of wood with what looked like two nails stuck through it. As the horrified keeper watched, Perry jabbed the nails again and again into his own eyes.

Shouting for help, the keeper struggled to wrangle the improvised weapon from the prisoner. Soon more keepers arrived with the prison physician, but they could barely restrain Perry, who seemed determined to keep stabbing his eyes even though the pain was so intense it had forced him to cry out. Eventually they wrestled him to the ground. Fearful that even in this state Perry might try to escape if taken to the hospital, the keepers pinned his arms and marched him, still struggling, to an isolated cell in a new prison building that was not yet occupied. There he was knocked out with chloroform.

Both his eyes were severely lacerated, but Conant Sawyer, the physician who had committed Perry, believed that the sight in one might be saved. When Perry woke he continued to struggle, so Sawyer kept him heavily sedated. By the end of September, Perry finally agreed to his eyes being treated and the physician was able to work without administering sedatives. Sawyer managed to preserve some of the sight in one eye but Perry was still in real distress, shouting his demands to anyone who came near. He wanted attention, he wanted better conditions and, above all, he wanted to go home. But he would not be going home, whatever he had hoped and wherever home might have been.

Perry had made a blinding machine with a piece of wood and two large saddler's needles, the sort used in the prison workshop. He had shown initiative and ingenuity in making use of everyday objects and material from his first escape attempt in 1892 to the sandbag episode a few weeks before this. Now, for reasons he would not reveal, he had turned this skill to terrible, self-destructive ends. As a result he was blind in one eye, had only limited vision in the other, and was soon to be declared insane once more.

On 1 November Dr Sawyer completed a new Certificate of Lunacy. In his accompanying letter to Dr Allison he noted that after a brief 'docile' period when he first returned to Auburn, Perry had been 'insolent, very talkative'. He went on to describe his unruliness and self-mutilation. But the horrors of Perry's condition had not diminished his physician's sense of humour, or of self-preservation, as he noted: 'In my last interview with him, he said that his next act would be to kill a prison official – the Deputy Warden and myself are special objects of his dislike and I have no special desire to gratify him in this direction.' The following day Perry was taken back to Matteawan.

Two months later he snapped again. But it was not a doctor or keeper that he attacked. Once again he tried to destroy his own eyes. This time he got hold of a small piece of broken glass, about the size of a 10-cent piece, placed it under the eyelid of his sighted eye, and rubbed until it was past saving. He had completed the terrible work begun in Auburn and would never see again. It was evidently the act of someone who was seriously disturbed, but why would a man who had only weeks before been planning an escape decide to destroy his own eyes?

Perry's first explanation, some time later, of why he had blinded himself was that he had been trying to win his freedom. He argued, in conversations leaked to the press, that because a blind man could pose no threat to society, the Governor might be merciful and set him free. It was, in other words, a logical, if terrible, extension of his compulsion to escape, to be free, at any cost. Was this the reason he did it? The trauma of prolonged sensory deprivation had clearly triggered a psychological collapse that made blinding himself seem a logical, if desperate, answer to his problems. If so, it did not work. Far from winning the Governor's sympathy, his act condemned him as hopelessly insane. And while he may have believed, at the time or in its aftermath, that he might gain something from his self-mutilation, the impulse behind it was certainly a distorted response to trauma.

There were undoubtedly other subconscious catalysts. Amelia Haswell, his 'Mother', was being tried, harassed and ridiculed for being in love with him. The analogy with Oedipus who blinded himself when he discovered that he had been incestuously in-volved with his own mother seems all too obvious. Haswell certainly believed that he had been affected by her situation, but it was probably part of a context of mounting pressure and increasing isolation that contributed to Perry slipping into another breakdown where his destructive logic of escape took control. Although it is often overlooked, Oedipus was marked for tragedy not just by his incestuous relationship with his mother but by his murder of his own father. It was not Amelia Haswell's love that Perry longed for, but his father's. The man who had rejected him in childhood continued to dominate his life. If he had once hoped to win his father's attention, even admiration, by robbing trains, now he had brought shame on him.

There may have been yet another catalyst. Self-blinding is almost totally confined to Christian cultures, and is associated with expiating sexual guilt by following, all too literally, scriptural commands to pluck out the offending eye. Predictably, it is Christian men in traditional communities who are racked with guilt about homosexuality who have most often destroyed their eyes. Could Perry have been reacting to guilt or shame about sexual relationships or encounters, either voluntary or forced, in his boyhood or more recently?

As always with Perry, the truth is elusive. His persistence in completing the blinding months later suggests that he was in the grip of a combination of guilt, self-loathing, fear and hope. It is quite possible that he was so desperate for freedom that he was ready to sacrifice his sight, and the blinding was, in one sense, an ironic victory. He had obliterated the sight of bars, uniforms and guards, and the men in power would never again be able to deprive him of daylight as a punishment. The dungeon would hold one less horror.

In the end, all the reasons for Perry's act will never be known. Throughout his life, he and others would reinvent that terrible moment to suit new purposes and arguments. The simplest and most convincing explanation was in a letter he wrote to Conant Sawyer. It suggests an extraordinary desire to exert control over his life, even at the most terrible cost, a desire that would define the rest of his life: 'I was born into the light of day, against my will of course. I now claim the right to put out that light.' As his relationships with his 'Mother' and father were threatened, Oliver Perry returned to the darkness of the womb to be reborn. And, most moving of all, he did so on his own birthday.

Today the Matteawan Asylum buildings are part of Fishkill prison, a medium-security institution surrounded by high fences whose razor-wire catches the light. The Superintendent's turreted quarters are boarded up, judged unsound, but some of the old wards and guards' quarters are still accessible. There are few objects left from the old asylum days, although correction officers remember finding strange medical instruments that were swiftly discarded or dispatched to museums. But one original feature is being recycled: the stained-glass windows that once decorated the Superintendent's rooms are being removed by inmates, under supervision, and placed in their dormitories. 'So the men can have a better view,' an officer remarked. Fishkill is also pioneering a new scheme called 'Puppies in Prison', and inmates can be seen walking dogs in the yard. In an ironic twist of history, the men in Perry's old 'home' are training seeing-eye dogs for the blind.

When Perry's blinding was leaked to the press, the reporters who had been mesmerized by Perry in the past thrilled their readers with accounts of his degeneration into madness. One insisted that 'sensible people are tired of Perry, and wish him to sink into oblivion where he belongs'. His shocking transformation seemed complete and as he struggled to cope with life as a blind man in an asylum, he was consigned not quite to oblivion but to near obscurity. The daring, debonair robber was forgotten and the blind 'lunatic' soon began to disappear as well.

In July 1896 Edward Clifford, who had captured Perry on the shore of the Hudson River, fell victim to his success. Clifford was popular, a decent, hard-working ex-policeman who had quit the force rather than get involved in corrupt politics. But he could not cope with the new prosperity and celebrity he acquired by capturing Perry. He lost his job because of excessive drinking and then shocked everyone by shooting the man who sacked him. Clifford was tried, found guilty of murder in the first degree, and sentenced to death by a familiar figure from the Jersey City legal farce, Justice Lippincott. His attorney, who had acted for Perry, tried once more to exploit loopholes in the law but the verdict was confirmed.

But there would be a long wait in jail for Edward Clifford, as appeals on the basis of temporary insanity continued, funded by popular benefits organized by none other than Chief Kelly. Clifford was finally hanged on 8 May 1900. If the four-year delay was long by the standards of the time, his execution was certainly cruel and unusual punishment: the drop failed to break Clifford's neck and it took him eighteen minutes to die of slow strangulation.

Perry also seems to have had a lasting impact on one of his Jersey cellmates. Paul Genz had finally been given the death sentence he had hoped for before Perry's arrival in the jail, but had rediscovered the will to live. Had his encounter with a man who fought so hard for freedom encouraged him not to give up so easily on life? His lawyers certainly used some of the same techniques as Perry's to get a reprieve, but it was only temporary. Just before he died, in 1897, like Perry he tried to stab himself in the eye. Was he genuinely deranged by fear or trying to feign insanity to save his life? In the end he faced the hangman calmly, but, like Edward Clifford, he took a long time to die: after the 'drop' he lived, hands clenching and unclenching, for fourteen minutes. Years later it was revealed that this was a signal to an opponent of capital punishment who wanted proof of the cruelty of hanging.

Perry, meanwhile, gradually regained some psychological balance. Dramatic as his breakdown had been, like the first episode that had taken him to Matteawan, it subsided. He would always be volatile, prone to violent mood swings and paranoia, but he remained intelligent, rational and capable. Little is known about his daily life in Matteawan but there are clear signs that he was not a broken man. He had occasional visits from Amelia Haswell, and he showed his determination once again, this time by overcoming the handicaps of blindness and imprisonment to write. He had always enjoyed writing when he was allowed pencil and paper. Now he had to rely on someone else to do the writing but when he was able to find a transcriber, he had an outlet that would become essential to his survival.

In October 1897, about two years after his return to Matteawan, a local newspaper published one of Perry's poems, noting that the one-time robber was 'considerable of a poet'. There is no surviving copy of the entire poem but a fragment remains on a torn newspaper. It told a conventional tale of a naughty boy's progress into a life of crime and ended with a defiant assertion that:

> I don't intend to serve this out
> Or even let despair,
> Deprive me of my liberty
> Or give me one grey hair.

The conclusion was intriguing. Surely as a blind man, certified once more as insane, he was not planning another escape? He was obviously not suicidal. So how was he planning to avoid serving out his sentence?

The plan soon became clear. Perry, the celebrity outlaw, hoped to use the press to engage public sympathy for an appeal to be released as a blind man who could do no harm. The poem was sent to the paper by one of Perry's supporters, probably Amelia Haswell, who also relayed his renewed allegations of abuses in the asylum. It was a sensible enough idea, but by now the press and public were more interested in Perry the character than Perry the protestor or Perry the poet. Since his return to the asylum he no longer made the front pages. Instead he was now a curiosity, almost a grotesque, to be paraded on the pages of the illustrated supplements published with weekend editions.

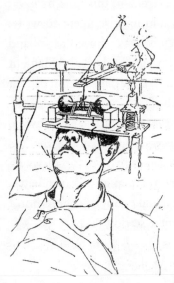

The *New York Tribune's* interpretation of Perry's 'Blinding Machine'.

The most extraordinary feature was in the *New York Tribune* in 1899. In it Perry described his blinding. Contrary to the official report, Perry claimed that he had devised an intricate blinding machine: 'I thought it out very carefully. I was very ingenious, even as a child.' He described constructing a blinding machine with wood, nails, cord and a candle, all smuggled into his cell or made from gifts, including a small dumbbell, meant for exercising, sent by friends. He had, he claimed, put sharpened nails through a piece of herring box, at exactly the right distance to pierce his eyes, and used the dumbbell to weight the board. Then he rigged up a pulley system above his bed that used a burning candle to release the weighted board so that it would drop into his eyes. Then, he said, he took some opium that he had obtained from a friend, lit the candle and waited for the machine to do its work.

Perry claimed that the Auburn officials had suppressed the story of his machine in order to avoid publicity. The apparatus, which he described in extraordinary detail, sounds impossible to construct in a prison, even for a man of Perry's evident ingenuity, but it is possible that he had managed to conceal the equipment he described in his cell, given the vagaries of prison security at the time. Even so, he was almost certainly embellishing the truth, hoping to turn the traumatic event that had labelled him a madman into a story of skill and daring, to recall, if not rival, those of his robberies. The compulsion to display his intelligence and skill that accompanied his masochistic recklessness was evidently as strong as ever. In the past it had charmed and impressed, now it merely seemed to prove his lunacy. The paper that printed his story even concluded that Perry's 'bump of self-esteem is, so to say, affected with elephantiasis, so that he loves notoriety with a consuming passion. And he has sought it in spectacular ways that would have fed the soul of Tom Sawyer.' Once Perry had been able to use the press even as it used him. The relationship was no longer mutually beneficial.

If Perry had not been judged an insane fantasist, his arguments easily dismissed as deranged, his criticisms of the institutions in which he was held might have found a more receptive audience. As the century drew to a close, an increasing number of people felt that the American dream was being turned to nightmare by unregulated business, political indifference and corruption, and a lack of welfare for the poor. New York's prisons came under mounting pressure from reformers, as the sheer number of convicts made primitive conditions intolerable. To some the prisons were a moral affront, to others examples of old-fashioned inefficiency in a system that gave powerful posts to friends and political allies rather than the able or experienced. Liberals and pragmatists alike pressed for curbs to the power of wardens and superintendents who ran them like private kingdoms. Over the coming decades there would be bitter battles over the correctional system, but in 1900 drastic measures were needed to avoid the immediate threat of violent insurrection.

Matteawan may have had medical aspirations, but it was no exception and by 1900 was a cause for real concern. Designed to hold 550 patients, it now housed 719. Henry Allison officially reported that conditions were dangerous: about 200 patients slept in corridors, and as there was inadequate housing for keepers, many were obliged to lodge outside, leading to security problems. Rumours of the state's solution, moving men to a new asylum within the grounds of Clinton prison in the village of Dannemora in the far north-east, just fifteen miles south of the Canadian border, made matters worse. Inmates dreaded being sent into what sounded like total isolation and panic ensued. In October a crowd of patients attacked their keepers in a mass escape attempt; although order was eventually restored, seven men got away. The following month, the first group of patients was transferred to the new asylum. This was designed to hold men who, like Perry, had been certified and, some might argue, driven insane while serving sentences; Matteawan would now only hold women and men judged insane at their trial. Sheer numbers meant that the transfer would be done in groups over the next year.

Perry, meanwhile, was continuing, with the assistance of friends, to seek public support for a pardon from the Governor. In 1901 a selection of his poetry was published in the *New York Journal*, William Randolph Hearst's rival to Pulitzer's *World*, the paper that had previously got the best Perry stories.

One poem, called 'Sweetheart', was addressed to an anonymous 'friend', a young woman whose identity is still unknown. The 'sweetheart' was possibly one of Perry's younger Christian supporters, possibly a friend of Amelia Haswell's, but she may have been an invention. Perry was still adept, even in an asylum, at tapping into the concerns of his audience. This poem neatly recalled the lost comforts of romance and home that Perry had once hinted at as the catalyst for his crimes:

> I often feign to be with thee,
> And to talk with thee and chat,
> But letters are no use to me,
> I am sightless – you know that,
> Yet the light I cannot moan,
> Nor your pretty eyes to meet,
> But break the bar and let me home,
> To your heart so pure and sweet.

The second poem was dedicated to his father:

> O father, list ye to my prayer,
> That tho' I oft did blunder
> I hope once more to be with thee,
> Ne'er again to break asunder.

While the sentiments, like those in the first poem, may have been designed to appeal to tender-hearted readers, there is a directness about the verse, despite its conventional language, that suggests it was heartfelt. Perry had angrily refuted rumours that his father had been terrified that his son would hunt him down when he escaped from Matteawan and clearly still yearned for his support.

The other poems were more explicitly concerned with his desire to be pardoned. One was addressed to the Governor, Republican Benjamin Odell, the other, the best of his poems, to an even higher power, calling on the 'Great Light divine' to:

> Flash down into this earthly hell
> Where lying brutes their libels tell
> And then, O, Christ, if it be right,
> Show me a friend of holy might
> Present some one from the outside world
> Who shall not cry, 'Demented, absurd'.

But demented and absurd was precisely what most people believed Oliver Perry to be, whatever his true condition. His campaign to be pardoned gained little momentum and a publicized fight with a fellow inmate damaged his cause. Its timing could not have been worse. Reformers had long argued that because when judged insane a convict could be held well beyond the end of his original sentence, even for life, he had little incentive to good behaviour. Finally, in 1901, a bill was passed to grant insane convicts the possibility of commutation of sentences. Perry's poems might have elicited public sympathy, but any official record of misconduct, even provoked, could ruin his chance of proving his sanity and winning his freedom.

The following spring he tried to make his case in person, when Governor Odell visited the asylum. Dr Allison met the Governor and his party, which included members of his family as well as state officials, at the ferry and escorted them on a tour of the institution. Just before his visit Odell had issued pardons for two Matteawan inmates, raising the hopes of many patients. The visitors asked to see the most notorious inmates, including Perry. Asked to present themselves for 'inspection', the patients seized their chance. First Quimbo Appo, a well-known old Chinese man, sent to Matteawan after a series of grisly murders, asked for a pardon so that he might return to China. When Odell refused, Appo reportedly became threatening and was dragged away. Perry tried a more diplomatic approach, shaking the Governor's hand and presenting a petition, signed by many of his supporters, for his release. Odell listened politely but, according to a report, 'left him with little hope'. The Governor finally fled when a Polish woman tried to show him the marks of the hypodermic needle on her arm that she claimed had driven her mad. Appo died in the institution, but some of the other hopeful patients did leave Matteawan before too long. On Wednesday, 5 June 1902, thirty-five men, including Perry, now thirty-seven years old, set out on the long railroad journey not to freedom, but to Danne-mora.

CHAPTER 17

Mountain Bughouse 216

THE RAILROAD journey upstate from Beacon to Plattsburgh, the nearest stop to the village of Dannemora, is truly spectacular. First the train runs alongside the wide Hudson River as it moves in stately fashion to the state capital, Albany, then passes through the foothills of the Adirondack wilderness until, hours later, it reaches the lakes of the North Country. It seems to move forward in space

but backward in time, as the buildings of successive generations give way to ancient forests and mountains, a landscape barely marked by its human inhabitants. Slowly but surely the train climbs until it is hugging a cliff wall high above the chain of lakes that mark the way to Canada. Nervous passengers, advised not to look down, stare ahead instead, only to see the front of the long train implausibly near the edge of the next bend in the cliff.

Plattsburgh sits on the last and largest lake, Champlain. On one side are the jagged heights of New York's High Peaks, on the other the blue Green Mountains of Vermont. It is the site of one of the decisive naval battles of the Revolutionary War, but here such recent events seem inconsequential. Rumours persist that a prehistoric creature still swims in the deeps of the lake. This is a New York as far removed from the metropolitan and industrial visions of the nineteenth and twentieth centuries as it is possible to imagine, but its sublime beauty has, inevitably, a dark side. As one nineteenth-century visitor commented, 'One is likely to become maudlin with the beauty of it all . . . to be possessed of an urgent desire to wander on and on.' Even today, an unprepared rover in these forests, the last remnant of those that once covered the whole state, may never return home.

When Perry and his fellow patients were transported here, the route would have been the same and the landscape similar. There are new houses, of course, but the wilderness is protected and few choose to live in such isolation all year round. In the long winters that can last into April, the temperature drops well below freezing; heavy snows cut off towns, villages and houses, and break power supplies, plunging modern residents back into an earlier way of life. Perry's train journey would have been much slower and far less comfortable. Even now there is only one train a day and one track in each direction, so a deer on the line or sudden bad weather can bring the service to a halt. A century ago visiting officials, with every comfort available to them, complained bitterly of the privations of a trip to Plattsburgh. Prisoners travelled in the most basic of conditions and even in the summer it would have been a miserable experience. To a blind man even the beauty of the landscape could offer no relief.

Dannemora State Hospital (Courtesy of Special Collections, Feinberg Library, State University of New York at Plattsburgh).

Dannemora was far away from the friends and supporters who helped Perry stay in touch with the free world. Visiting Matteawan may not always have been easy for Amelia Haswell and her fellow reformers, but the trip to the distant Adirondacks was daunting indeed. Perry knew that he was facing the greatest isolation of his life. The reputation of Clinton prison, within whose grounds his new asylum stood, was fearsome, as its nicknames reveal: 'Little Siberia', 'the Northern Bastille', the 'Dark Hole of Calcutta'. Since the prison opened in 1845, its remote location had fostered a regime that seemed indifferent to regulation. Rumours of terrible abuses led to investigations that would culminate in 1903 with the state hiring Pinkerton agents to go undercover as prisoners. The threat of ending up in Clinton had discouraged Perry from turning himself in after the first robbery and now he would be doubly confined within its grounds. Some may have found a bleak justice in this eventual journey.

Clinton, today still a maximum-security prison housing more than 2,500 men, is one of the most imposing correctional institutions in the United States. To those outside the state its name has little resonance, but once seen it is never forgotten. At night its lights shine clear across to the neighbouring state of Vermont, in daylight it is equally daunting. Clinton's sheer size and immense, solid perimeter wall, totally enclosing the world of the prison, manage to upstage its dramatic backdrop of dark wooded mountains and dwarf the small village of Dannemora that grew up around it. Clinton's convicts once laboured in rich iron ore mines, while the village people found work in the prison and later in the asylum. The work was hard and poorly paid. Even in the 1940s asylum attendants received low wages and only two weeks' vacation a year. Extraordinarily, they were obliged to draw lots for when they could take it, with losers having to take precious holidays in deepest winter.

In 1896 the Superintendent of Prisons, the Warden of Sing-Sing and Henry Allison of Matteawan had visited Dannemora and chosen it as the site for a new asylum. It is hard now to imagine how such a remote location, far from most patients' families and friends, can have seemed a good choice, but the decision was both well intentioned and expedient. Like Matteawan, it was a rural, supposedly restful, location, with cold, clear air that gave Clinton

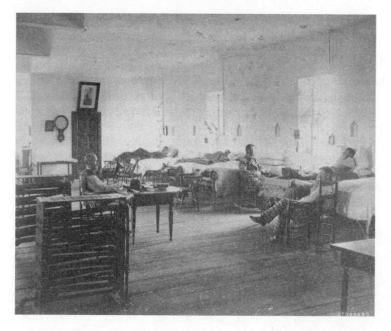

A Dannemora Ward during Perry's time there (Courtesy of Special Collections, Feinberg Library, State University of New York at Plattsburgh).

the highest survival rates in the state of prisoners with tuberculosis. It also had a supply of free convict labour to build the new institution.

The completed asylum was celebrated in the press as 'A Comfortable and Ornamental Structure, and Credit to the State'. Its opulent entrance is unchanged, with an elegant hallway and sweeping staircase of dark, highly polished wood. An early visitor could have easily felt that he or she was entering a well-appointed retreat. But the building that is now a medium-security annexe to the main prison was then known as the 'mountain bughouse' and the bugs' accommodation was less than salubrious. Today most of the men sleep in dormitories, as if they were in a particularly shabby boarding school, but some, such as sex offenders and others who need to be segregated for their own safety, still inhabit the 'rooms' that once held the criminal insane: stone cells with high windows that even now, with heating, are chilly reminders of life beyond the polished surface. Like Matteawan, this institution has moved on, but its past is visible in odd corners. Prisoners queue to see the doctor outside cold tiled rooms where the original inmates were once 'treated'. In the basement is a row of bare stone cells, formerly used to hold the most unruly men. Nearby stands a large steel cage with wide-spaced bars. Now it stores broken furniture, but its design suggests it would have been ideal for administering the notorious water treatment used across the state in Perry's day. Here men who could not be controlled in any other way could, like Perry when he attacked James Shaw in Auburn, be blasted with high-pressure water hoses until they were subdued. The force drove men against the bars and made many lose control of their bowels.

Perry should logically have disappeared in Dannemora, as he all but did in Matteawan. Few traces of convicts declared insane were preserved and most that were are forbidden to the public. But digging in the Dannemora archives revealed a case file full of Perry's correspondence and writings. There are letters from supporters and government officials, and on dozens of pieces of paper, from neat lined sheets to small torn scraps, and always written in pencil, Oliver Perry's own writings. Unlike the letter from Lyons, these are not, of course, in his own handwriting. As in Matteawan, he dictated all his letters and poems to other inmates, whose varying degrees of literacy are poignantly revealed. One or two wrote in careful copperplate, but most struggled to spell even simple words and were defeated by Perry's sometimes ambitious vocabulary. Intriguingly, each note is signed 'Oliver C. Perry' with a similar flourish and large, proud capitals, suggesting the blind prisoner was still determined to sign his own name. Although Dannemora threatened Perry with the greatest isolation of his life, it has left the fullest record of his thoughts, revealing a man of extraordinary determination and spirit.

If the Matteawan authorities breathed a sigh of relief when Perry went north, those in Dannemora may have had greater confidence that they could cope. The new building was not overcrowded and was certainly less vulnerable to escape attempts. And Perry seemed to be a spent force. Times had changed, new stories occupied the press, and how much trouble could one blind madman cause? The staff in the new hospital would also have been well prepared for Perry, as their first Superintendent was Dr Robert Lamb, the physician and amateur photographer from Matteawan. Dr Lamb had done rather well for himself. As well as being promoted to the new post, he was highly respected in state government circles. In the summer of 1902, when Perry arrived, he was travelling in Europe for the New York Department of Prisons, to explore new approaches to criminal identification. He went first to Paris to study under Alphonse Bertillon, the deviser of the Bertillon method of identification by measurement, then on to England to research the even newer technique of reading fingerprints. But if the Superintendent and his staff assumed that Perry would be easier to manage than he had been in his previous institutions, they were badly mistaken.

The person who knew Perry best, who had stood by him through all his, and her own, trials and tribulations, was Amelia Haswell. Determined to bridge the great distance between them, she wrote to Dannemora with extraordinary regularity: long letters to Perry with religious cards, newspaper clippings and brief notes to the Superintendent accompanied by money to buy 'comforts' for her friend. Her greatest gift, was, in her eyes, the reminder of his hopes for a better life to come, but she did all she could to make his present life more bearable. Every couple of weeks she sent money for small items, each winter she sent money for flannel underwear or blankets to help him survive the terrible cold, and each Christmas she sent a gift. All too often these were judged inappropriate and returned, much to his, and her, disappointment. But it was her letters, often the only friendly contact Perry had, that were his real lifeline. Communication with the outside world was one of the most precious privileges for the men in Dannemora. It was also one of the easiest to control and silence from a patient often meant that the privilege had been withdrawn as a punishment. Perry's silences could last for many months and his friend's ensuing anxiety was exacerbated by the distance between them.

Amelia Haswell was neither rich nor in good health, but she was determined to visit Perry in his first summer in Dannemora. Perhaps unwisely, she wrote to him about her plan, only to find that ill health prevented her. Her own eyes had become diseased, and one was removed that year in an emergency operation. The experience deepened her sympathy for Perry, but her understanding was no consolation. Although she reassured him she would make the journey at a later date, and did manage to visit him some years later, his disappointment when the visit was postponed was acute. As Amelia Haswell knew, to a man with little to look forward to, and who had felt betrayed and unwanted since infancy, few things hurt as much as a broken promise. There is no record of how Perry responded to this disappointment. But he was already preoccupied with the miseries of his new home and about to embark on a potentially fatal campaign against one aspect of the Dannemora regime: food.

Food had long been something of an obsession of Perry's. After a childhood of neglect, poverty and abuse, he was always anxious, sometimes paranoid, about what he ate. Food had been the trigger of many incidents in Auburn and Matteawan and in Dannemora it was the catalyst for his next dramatic act. It started with his usual, and undoubtedly accurate, complaints about his rations. Food in all prisons was bad: often stale, sometimes maggoty, and rarely nourishing. Organized and casual 'scams' meant that better items might be creamed off, while contamination by staff or inmates was an ever-popular trick.

One of Perry's more light-hearted criticisms was a sarcastic four-page long 'Bill of Fare' describing a week's meals. This included breakfasts of 'cracked rice mush with watered molasses' or 'cornmeal mush', dinners of 'pea soup well watered', 'beef stew with mighty little meat' and 'fresh fish and unpared potatoes no longer than hen's eggs. No gravy and about two mouths of fish', and suppers of 'Apple sauce well watered', and 'five prunes floating in water'. 'The meals', Perry concluded, 'consist of mush, mush, mush, or slush, slush, slush.'

While few can have relished their rations, Perry had additional reasons for complaint. He had been suffering for years from the combined effects of the rupture discovered soon after his arrival in Auburn, and of later beatings, that made it hard for him to digest many foods. As a blind man he also had physical diffi-culties in eating some foods, and an increased vulnerability that gave him a deep suspicion of what he was eating and a desperate desire to get some control over it. Using his ability to turn other people's logic to his own advantage, as he had in court and in the press, he argued that as he had been judged insane, and so in need of care, he should be given better food than that provided for ordinary prisoners. No concessions were made, so, convinced that he had nothing to lose, he took a dramatic step. On 19 November 1903 he announced that unless his requests for better food were granted he would stop eating altogether. The authorities refused to listen, so he refused all food. Oliver Perry was on hunger strike.

CHAPTER 18

'When I am yelling for freedom'

DAYS PASSED, Perry began to weaken, and still he refused to eat. Without food, death would be a certainty before long. But was he really determined to die rather than compromise? He was certainly not suicidal. A man like Perry, as he had proved when he blinded himself, could have found a quicker way to die. There was no audience watching or waiting for the outcome. Although he was genuinely angry about the conditions he and his fellow patients endured, unusually, given his past mania for publicity, he did not seem to be trying to attract the attention of the press or the public. In his letters to Amelia Haswell and others he made no reference to the hunger strike as a public protest, only mentioning the particular concerns he wanted addressed by his keepers. Just as his reasons for blinding himself remained unclear, so Perry's motives in taking his hunger strike so far were never fully explained, but he was undoubtedly driven by the reckless, masochistic impulsiveness that characterized his adult life. He was trying to assert his will, at any cost.

In years to come similar situations would test prison authorities across the world. Some prisoners have stopped eating as a suicidal protest, refusing to sustain a life no longer worth living.

Others, like the British suffragettes and Irish Republicans, have used their own bodies as weapons in a battle for political change. Today, the legal and ethical dilemmas of treating a prisoner who refuses food are complicated by the gaze of the media, but the central question remains: can someone be forced to live? In the closed world of the asylum in 1903, the doctors had an answer. When Perry was near death, they strapped him to a table, pushed a tube up his nostril and poured a mixture of eggs and milk into his stomach.

When it was clear that the doctors could end his hunger strike by force, Perry changed tactics. He was determined to win some control over his life, so if his food was served according to his requirements, he would eat. If not, he insisted, the doctors would have to tube-feed him or watch him die. In effect he forced his own force-feeding. From his cell he issued constant written requests and complaints. Sometimes he included his fellow inmates, with whom he seems to have been quite popular, as he had been in the past, in his requests. But usually his demands were personal: Oliver Perry was still a determined individualist. His demands often read like an imperious customer dealing with room service in a bad hotel. He refused food because it was inferior to that served to the keepers, or had been tampered with, such as milk that he claimed was watered down after the cream had been skimmed off for the staff. He rejected food that was stale, like a cake sent by Amelia Haswell and delivered so late it had dried up.

Sometimes he specified what he would like to eat, in bills of fare that read like poignant reminders of real food he had once enjoyed: '*Breakfast*. Two hard fried eggs turned over; and boiled or fried potatoes or hash. *Dinner*. Fried Beefsteak, or carved

October 27, 1904.
Oliver Curtis Perry
Diet.

Three thin slices of warm buttered toast that are not sour or heavy. Two bowls of hot milk in a measure accompanied by a bowl for drinking purposes, and two pieces of butter at each meal with the following—
Breakfast—Two hard fried eggs turned over and hash or potatoes with gravy when prepared.
Dinner:—Beefsteak or Carved Roast Beef or Fresh Fish with potatoes and gravy. also a little turnip or beans or maccaroni or cabbage in order to get the vinegar which they call for.
Supper:— Two hard fried eggs turned over, and fried potatoes or hash, and sauce when prepared.
In God we trust.
O. C. Perry.

One of Perry's bills of fare.

Roast Beef, or fresh fish together with boiled or mashed potato and gravy. Also macaroni and beans when prepared. *Supper.* Two hard fried eggs turned over; and fried potatoes or hash.'

Only rarely did Perry win any concessions from his doctors and keepers and many notes revealed the harsh reality of his situation. He often begged the doctors to warm through the mixture that they pumped through his nose into his stomach or to reduce its volume so that it caused him less pain. Although sometimes he ate regular food in his room from a metal plate, and his weight remained quite stable, Perry was forcibly tube-fed, sometimes for weeks at a time, for the rest of his long years in Dannemora.

His attempt to take control of his own life was not confined to eating. After years of complaining about being forcibly drugged, he tried to manipulate the use of medication. He warned his doctors that if his suffering became too much to bear, he would shout all night until they administered a knockout injection and gave him some 'oblivion'. As with the tube-feeding, he tried to turn punishment into treatment on demand. Some months later he extended his campaign even further. Insisting that as a man judged 'insane' he should not be forced to wear the degrading clothing of a prisoner, particularly distressing for a man once known for his style, he tore off all his clothes and demanded decent attire. When this was refused he went naked, wrapping himself in a blanket only when visitors arrived, anticipating by over half a century the actions of political prisoners in Northern Ireland. Occasionally he would wear underclothes, if he felt that he had been well treated. Going naked was no casual gesture. Perry was housed in a room with no heating and in winter the temperature was well below zero, day and night.

It would be hard to argue that a man who imposed such a regime on himself was sane, but his writings, preserved by the authorities he fought, reveal that while he was clearly prone to paranoid fears and compulsions, his intellect and reason were as sharp as ever and he had sensitivity and subtlety as well as a violent temper. His behaviour also prefigured that of some more recent prisoners who, after extreme bouts of destructive-ness and delusion, have, in better surroundings, recovered completely.

Coincidentally, just weeks after New York's greatest train robber started his hunger strike, Thomas Edison, inventor of the electric lights that had illuminated Utica in 1891, thrilled America with the first real 'feature film' to be shown in the nation's vaudeville theatres: *The Great Train Robbery*. At twelve minutes, this was the longest, most dramatic moving picture ever, telling the story of bandits robbing a train. While the action took place in the 'West', it was filmed in studios and on the railroads in New York and New Jersey. Edison publicists boasted that New York's own 'frontier' train robberies could only enhance the film's appeal to eastern audiences. A dramatic scene in which a robber fired his gun straight at the shocked but delighted audience showed just how powerful this new medium would be, with crime a favourite subject as it had been in the dime novels of the 1890s.

It was, of course, one Perry would never experience. Life in an asylum for a blind man must have been at best tedious, at worst terrifying. There was no work or education and, although he made some friends, he was frequently housed with the most irrational and disturbed men. But, with difficulty, he had sustained his own love of writing. He was dependent on others to read and write for him, and the only way to get another patient to do so was by paying him with tobacco. When this worked, he could hear letters and books and dictate his own thoughts. But when his keepers or doctors wanted to punish him, they could easily stop him buying tobacco, or simply lock his door. His supporters, and state officials, repeatedly advised the doctors that letting someone read and write for him could only help alleviate his situation and their own, giving him some mental stimulation to distract him from his complaints. One governor even sent word that Perry should be allowed notepaper to write to him. But time and again, the response to his unruly behaviour was to deprive him of this outlet. The officials' actions may well be understandable – Perry must have been infuriating – but they made the problem worse.

His many notes and letters, from the periods when he was allowed to write, testify to his desperate need to communicate, to find a voice that could not be silenced by drugs or double-doored cells. He also continued to write poems, which he had transcribed into a little book that was his prize possession. The poems were generally protests or appeals for sympathy. Some were religious in theme, with conventional messages of promised renewal and redemption designed to appeal to his supporters. Some expressed more personal and tangible hopes.

One written in 1904, called 'My Prospective Friend', was addressed to a new physician, Dr Charles North, who had recently arrived in Dannemora from a post in Matteawan. The physician was reported to be a fine amateur actor and shared Perry's love of music: an accomplished violinist, he even started a patients' orchestra. If Perry had known him in Matteawan, he gave no hint of their relationship in his poem, but, as he had so often, he was pinning his hopes on one man:

> Oh! Doctor Nord; if thou only
> Let me tell my stomach's tail [sic]
> It will reveal how very lonely;
> Veryly [sic] do I moan and wail;
> Ere long I pray that thou may find
> Room in thy heart for one whose [sic] blind.

The Patients' Orchestra at Dannemora (Courtesy of Special Collections,
Feinberg Library, State University of New York at Plattsburgh).

Dr North's reaction to his welcoming poem is not known but he
would occupy a place in Perry's thoughts for over a decade. In the
coming years Perry would repeatedly accuse him of both systematic corruption and personal vindictiveness, and North would
block all attempts to review Perry's case. None of Perry's accusations was investigated and many of North's practices, that seem
harsh or insensitive today, were common at the time. Two
examples reveal North's rigidity and Perry's frustration.

First, a few years after his arrival, North refused Amelia Haswell's request to be allowed to send Perry a mandolin for Christmas.
She and some of his other friends hoped would that this would help
occupy and cheer Perry who, like the physician, had always loved
music. But North was unmoved. Perry remembered the decision for
the rest of his life. Years later he reminded his friend that the
Superintendent allowed some patients to buy beer 'but when I was
anxious to drink in a few notes from a mandolin which you and

others desired to send me, oh! that was different and yet he has never suggested any occupation for the mind'. To mark another Christmas, Amelia Haswell hoped to send Perry a ring. In her accompanying letter to Dr North she acknowledged her impulse might seem odd, 'but when you consider how few things one can send a blind man, and knowing how much he used to prize a ring and as some one suggested it, I acted upon it. It is inexpensive (not solid) and I thought whether in the circumstances you might allow it.' North again refused. He may simply have been following the letter of the law, but his decisions appeared insensitive and short-sighted to Amelia Haswell who believed some kindness would encourage Perry to cooperate with his doctors. To Perry they appeared to be the work of a vindictive man bent on persecuting him.

Returned letter from Amelia Haswell.

Whatever the rights and wrongs of both men's behaviour, Perry's 'prospective friend' swiftly became his most hated 'adversary', a personification of the brutality, indifference and cruelty of the system. To make matters worse for Perry, towards the end of 1904 Henry Allison died and Robert Lamb returned to

Matteawan as Superintendent, leaving a vacancy in Dannemora that Charles North hoped to fill.

Perry's fear about North's likely promotion was evident in a letter to Amelia Haswell, urging her to start a new petition to the Governor for his parole to a regular asylum near his friends. Amelia Haswell was working hard on his behalf, sending stories to the press. As his hunger strike had changed into a long-term campaign, Perry had turned his attention to getting out of Dannemora. But, aware of his damaged reputation, he had evidently decided that 'escape' to an asylum for free men was his only real hope. He wanted her to publicize it in the press because, as he noted with his ever acute understanding of the power of the press, 'President Roosevelt says that the only way to work quick reforms is through the public newspapers and he is right.' By this time, even Cole Younger, a killer as well as robber, had been paroled and pardoned. But he, unlike Perry, had been a model prisoner, had never complained and had certainly never been certified insane. Perry's letter, accompanied by a poem that combined religious sentiments with scathing references to North's 'crooks', was annotated 'Not mailed owing to the many false statements referring to other patients, which if true would have no relation to Perry's affairs. C.H.N.'

But Amelia Haswell kept trying on his behalf, even telling the *New York Evening World* that he had blinded himself for her sake. She claimed that for a man who had always chosen an outdoor life, being confined was torture, and whenever he glimpsed the sky he was driven to attempt to escape. If he could no longer see, he would no longer be tempted; if no longer tempted, he could not disappoint her again. The story was a 'hook' to draw press and public attention to Perry's present situation explained in an excerpted letter from the prisoner.

He described a brutal and mean regime, with men stealing blankets from one another in order to endure the harsh winter conditions. In a move calculated to appeal to Christian reformers, he also drew attention to the lack of religious services for many months, because the attendants used the only suitable room for their weekly dances instead. The image of attendants dancing while their damaged charges were deprived of the consolations of religion was surely bound to appal the respectable reader. 'Is this a hospital in reality?' asked Perry. 'Shame upon all Christian taxpayers who know and still allow this degrading and brutalizing mismanagement to continue.' The stories were most probably true, but, as ever, Perry did not miss a trick in spinning them to appeal to his readers. He had declared years before that he was no longer a believer, but he knew that his most faithful supporters were.

Amelia Haswell kept trying to explain Perry's behaviour to his doctors in the hope they would understand and help him. 'Oliver is naturally quick and fiery and impulsive, and his intentions might be the best, but when brought to the test of patient waiting and forbearance, in this he was sorely lacking, not having learned self-control in his past life it is not so easy now.' 'This would be no evidence of insanity to me,' she added, rather naively, 'for I know it was his natural temperament.' She was at pains to show she was sympathetic to the doctors. 'I can understand how Oliver might be a very trying patient – but when I attempt to put myself in his place, imagine my being blind among lunatics, and no way of diverting my mind, it would be enough to drive a sane man insane.' She repeatedly, but unsuccessfully, urged the Superintendent to try a new approach: 'Such men are used to cuffs and blows and curses, but kindness in time I believe will touch the hardest heart.'

Whatever the miseries of his life, and the restrictions imposed by his doctors, Perry had retained three distinctive characteristics from happier days: a love of music, a concern for his personal appearance, and an almost childish sweet tooth. Inmates were generally allowed to receive carefully vetted gifts, and also money to purchase goods through the steward. Amelia Haswell duly sent money, usually $2, every few weeks, so that Perry could do so. Many of his requests were refused, but they reveal his tastes. At the end of 1904, for example, he hoped to purchase a 'twenty-five cent harmonica made by M. Hohner in A or D key', 'granulated sugar', a 'pound of raisins', and a 'pound of stick peppermint candy'. In a later note, that may reveal the heightened senses blindness brought, he asked for '2 jars of scented cold cream – 20c, 2 envelopes of sen sen [breath perfumes] – 10c, 4lbs of roasted peanuts for 50c, shiff of keenans [tobacco] – 20c, 2 plugs of Climax – 20c, 1lb of B & J peppermint drops – 20c, 2 coconuts, Adams wintergreen flavored gum – 25c.'

Perry's sweet tooth, and the occasional treats he was allowed, contributed to another of his problems. He had been suffering from the sharp torment of constant toothache for years. Campaigns at the time to allow prisoners to purchase toothpowder show that dental hygiene was non-existent in correctional institutions. Eventually his teeth were in such a bad condition that eating, even when he wanted to, was a near impossibility. Amelia Haswell offered to pay for them to be replaced with dentures. After protracted negotiations with the dentist who worked for the hospital, a set was produced, but it was shoddy and ill-fitting. Perry was infuriated, but retained his sense of humour. He wrote to the dentist, accusing him of using inferior materials, knowing that when the dentures broke 'you could rest securely in your position as a respectable citizen and say "Oh! I can't help it, the poor fellow is crazy and has probably been trying to take a piece out of his iron bedstead, or something of that sort."' In the end Amelia Haswell demanded her money back and Perry's teeth were forgotten.

But Perry had also retained his ability to make friends among his fellow prisoners. One wrote to him from New York City:

Friend Oliver,

I wrote you in a poem that I would remember you. I am out, and as I thought about my promise to-day, I count [sic] help writing this letter. Is Miss A. Haswell sticking to you still, I know she cares a good deal about you and I hope you still respect her in your heart.

How is Supt. Lamb and Dr. North, the nurses, attendants and the boys. How is your health and let me know if possible everything worth knowing about yourself.

Friend Oliver I am in good health, getting stout and doing well. 'The unexpected often happens' and I experienced it as never before when I was told to pack up and be good to myself. Well, I never in all my life felt so happy; liberty was sweeter, the air was better, food tasted different, and in fact nature seemed a smiling; everything was good with the exception of the Devil, the same old Satan.

Cheer up and be of good courage, don't worry, for you ought to know worry has not done anybody good. Oliver the unexpected in your life may happen some day, if not in this world perhaps in the next. I hope it will be for the better. Good old New York town has changed greatly; for old time sake I took a car to see the city; first I went through the subway by local and express, then I took a ride on the Third Ave. Elevated Road, then the surface roads as the Third Ave., Madison Ave, and horse car. One fine day I went to Coney Island, and I must say it was greatly changed for the better. Gee if I told you one quarter of what I saw it would fill a good sized book. Dear old Coney Island was still waiting for me, and I was glad to see it looking so well. I enjoyed myself greatly and left early, because my money gave out. I could stay there all day, it was so good, with the bands of music playing and the people so happy also so many new things that was interesting and your money going, gee it was all to the good.

Not wishing to bore you with a long letter I will cut it short by wishing you God's luck, also all them that I have mentioned in this letter.

I remain,

your friend,

Hyman.

Hyman Epstein had been Perry's fellow inmate and, it seems, friend, although this is the only record of their relationship. Epstein's own story was a strange one. In 1901 the twenty-one-year-old Jewish New Yorker had been sentenced to two years in prison. In Auburn he converted to Christianity but his behaviour was interpreted as religious mania and he was declared insane. After a spell in Dannemora where he befriended Perry, he was sent, at the end of his sentence, to the asylum on Ward's Island in Manhattan where he was to be held indefinitely. His family made no attempt to aid him as they refused to accept his conversion as the act of a sane man, while the asylum authorities insisted that he was insane because he claimed to have 'seen Jesus Christ'. Epstein seemed doomed to remain incarcerated indefinitely. So one September morning in 1903 he slipped away from the guards, crept to the riverbank and started swimming across the East River to freedom. Powerfully built, he was making good progress against a swift current when a policeman in a patrol boat spotted him. Assuming he was an unfortunate sailor who had fallen overboard, the patrolmen tried to rescue him. Epstein attempted to dodge the boat but eventually gave himself up.

He was taken to the police court in Harlem, where he explained his story to the magistrate. For the first time, almost miraculously, somebody in authority believed him. The magistrate, impressed by his rationality, declared that it was an outrage that he had been locked up in an asylum. It was, he said, no crime for a sane man to attempt to escape from such confinement. The asylum physician's explanation did not impress the magistrate: 'I have seen a number of religious persons who have contended that they have seen Christ, and they were not insane, either.' He declared Epstein sane, and announced that he would spend his own money to help him gain his freedom. Eventually a Supreme Court writ was issued against the asylum to show cause for Epstein's detainment, and in due course he left Ward's Island a free man.

Perry may have lost a friend but he was now just as determined to escape. In June 1906 he wrote a letter of appeal to the new Governor, Republican Frank Higgins, accompanied by an acrostic poem called 'Chief Executive'. Composing acrostics, a form he used many times, was quite a feat for a blind man who relied on the help of men whose literacy was rarely developed. The challenge was clearly something Perry relished but this time the ambition of the poem's content, begging for a chance to prove his worth as a reformed man, was let down by the form. In an unusual lapse, either he or his transcriber thought 'Governor' only had one 'r', and the first letters of each line consequently spelled out 'Honorable Govenor [sic] Higgins'. What Higgins would have made of the poem, or appeal, will never be known, as the authorities decided it was unacceptable and marked it 'Don't Send'. Undaunted, Perry kept up a sustained campaign to convince politicians and government officials that his case should be reviewed, writing to successive governors and members of the Commission in Lunacy responsible for overseeing the state's institutions. Just as each new doctor would receive a poem, so each time a new man took up public office, he would hear from Dannemora State Hospital 216.

Perry's keepers heard his complaints even more loudly, as a special Fourth of July poem called 'A Parody' revealed. Written to be sung to the music of 'Marching through Georgia', it commemorated a protest that Perry seems to have particularly enjoyed:

How the turkeys gobbled when they heard me yell so loud;
How the Doctors wondered that I was never cured;
How the village people all gathered in a crowd
When I was yelling for freedom.
(Chorus)
Hurrah! Hurrah! come give a shout with one;
Hurrah! Hurrah! I know you would be free,
And so I hope to make it, to live in good old Troy.
For I am working so hard boys.

How the 'Bugs' did curse that time O yes it was a fright;
How they damned and double-damned the man who's out of
   sight;
How they would have choked me all in my sightless plight
When I was yelling for freedom.
(Chorus)

How the Doctors suffer when they see one with a friend;
How they long to queer me when money they do send;
How they try to starve me, no solace to extend
When I am yelling for freedom.
(Chorus)

Someone, presumably a doctor, wrote on the poem, in red ink,
'Illustrative of Perry's Egotism'.

CHAPTER 19

'O God, how much longer?'

IN AUGUST 1907 the men of Dannemora rioted for the first time. Only five years after opening, the asylum was already so overcrowded that some of the most dangerous men were housed in a dormitory, allowing them to collaborate in planning what turned into a desperate siege. They improvised weapons by getting hold of some sash weights and breaking up several beds and a steam radiator. Guards used ammonia fumes, then resorted to turning the high-pressure water hose on men who appeared through the windows, and finally to shooting. The order was only to kill if absolutely necessary, but when the riot was finally quelled, it was discovered that one patient, Isaac Dubois, had died from gunshot wounds. In the past, Perry would surely have been at the centre of any dramatic event, but this time he was not involved. A blind man would have had little chance of taking part in such a protest, and Perry spent his time composing letters and poetry to demand a better life.

Sometimes his protests were personal: on 1 January 1907 he dictated a mordant, and prophetic, acrostic spelling out 'Unhappy New Year'. But increasingly he attacked the asylum regime more formally. That same year he sent a letter via a local clergyman to the Reverend John Warren, Amelia Haswell's brother-in-law, who, he hoped, would in turn forward it to the new Governor, Charles Hughes. The elaborate chain was devised to overcome possible censorship. His complaints now were not only about brutality or cruelty, but about serious financial corruption, and, for a certified lunatic, he displayed inside knowledge of the institution as well as a keen understanding of the contemporary political context.

He was clearly anxious about how he would be read – 'I shall try not to make a misstatement as I realize that it would reflect upon my sanity or veracity' – but adamant in his critique of conditions and corruption. Perry evidently hoped that Governor Hughes, in his opinion 'no machine man', would condemn the doctors who 'graft at the expense of their patients'. After cataloguing petty abuses and contrasting asylum conditions with those in the neighbouring prison, he turned to accusations of corruption, from 'petty graft' to serious allegations.

He claimed that 'a summer residence at the lake' had been 'finished off with lumber from our new chapel and dining room' and 'provisioned from our store room to feed Supt. Collins, Dr Lamb and all their friends who wish to visit these mountains'. Hospital employees were too busy working on this camp to look after patients, he wrote, because 'Dr North's principal desire is to make a good showing before the Albany authorities and at the same time graft for himself.' Although the Adirondack forests were under pressure, because of the demand for newsprint, 'camps', lavish vacation homes that combined rural style and real luxury, were increasingly fashionable as retreats for Vanderbilts and Rockefellers. Some survive today as expensive hotels and restaurants serving local delicacies like wintergreen ice-cream. The irony of Perry's observations about the use of prison timber and labour to build such a 'residence' was, in the circumstances, remarkably understated.

While the Dannemora doctors fed their horses on good oats, wrote Perry, their patients lived on 'mush' and 'like Oliver Twist the mush eaters are crying for more'. He offered a catalogue of petty actions by the doctors that seem trivial, but must have seemed unbearably cruel to men with little pleasure in life. One prohibited gifts or purchases of handkerchiefs or soap because he considered the official provision adequate, and of cheese, because 'he don't like the smell'. Another banned peanuts because 'once upon a time some unfortunate happened to drip a few peanut shells upon the floor'.

Corruption and indifference, Perry insisted, had led to the neglect of patients. In the hospital the already basic bathroom facilities had been allowed to fall into disrepair, 'so now we have but two seats and one urinal for about a hundred men [in his section]. Sometimes a man will urinate in the sink where we must stand to wash.' One urinal had, he claimed, been removed and installed in the summer camp, while broken combs provided for general use were rarely replaced, a 'brush hung for over two years until the hairs wore down to the wood', and only 'two roller towels for so many men, some of whom are diseased, makes it seem very unsanitary'. While he dwelt at length on the degradations of poor hygiene, the terseness of the ex-reformatory boy's most serious allegation is perhaps telling: 'There is little classification and young fellows from Elmira reformatory are herded in dormitories with old-time criminals who frequently seduce the weaker ones under the promise of candy, etc. I know several who commit unnatural crimes in two and three ways during the day as well as at night.'

Perry seemed genuinely concerned about the situation of all the men in Dannemora and his letter reads as a heartfelt protest about conditions and corruption rather than a calculated pretext for a private plea. He had clearly managed to follow what was happening in American politics and saw his situation as part of a greater picture. He was particularly impressed by President Roosevelt, who had made some moves against systematic corruption. His admiration for the President may have been increased by the many parallels in their lives. Roosevelt may have been born into affluence rather than poverty, but he was, like Perry, a puny child who made himself an athlete, an easterner with a taste for western adventure, and a man of charisma, courage and determination. He also happened to be a champion of simplified spelling.

But the conclusion to Perry's protest letter was deeply personal and concerned with the psychological and physical torments of his daily life: 'O God, how much longer? I am harassed by day and haunted in my nightly dreams. I pace up and down and sing or chant in order to keep from talking to myself about my troubles.' His mental misery was exacerbated by his physical conditions: 'I have been not let out in God's sunshine for over four years yet Dr Macdonald will not leave my door open as he does that of others so that I can get some reading done [by allowing a patient to enter and read to him]. No warmth will reach me in this cold room and I feel the strain upon my mind.' He ended by begging his friend to send the letter to the Governor, but also with a more immediate request, to help him get a hot-water radiator that he could use to warm through the tube-feeding mixture and ease his aching stomach and kidneys.

It is difficult to imagine what the Governor might have made of the letter. Hughes was a tough but progressive Republican, described by Roosevelt as 'the bearded iceberg'. But Perry's complaints would go unread. A year later John Warren was writing to Dr North for news of Perry, as he had heard nothing from him.

Perry's writings, by and large, make depressing reading, in the topics and their tone. His complaints were usually justified but his own inflexible attitude and refusal to conform meant that he and his keepers were almost always at loggerheads and his harsh, self-imposed regime of near-starvation and nakedness took its toll. It is easy to believe that he was a broken man, old before his time, sustained only by a determination to beat the system. But two poems, still sealed up in small envelopes in his file nearly a hundred years later, reveal with almost shocking clarity that he was not always gloomy or hopeless. They were written not long after a visit by Amelia Haswell and some of her friends from Troy, and were confiscated and sealed by disapproving staff in Dannemora. The first was marked 'Obscene Poem, given to Dr R. S. Lepes, September 11 1907':

> There once was a pretty young miss
> Who thought it the acme of bliss
> To frig herself silly
> With the stem of a lily
> Then sit on a sunflower to piss.

The records reveal nothing, but this tiny scrap of grubby humour suggests a side to Perry that would otherwise have been totally obscured. Was the poem specially designed to impress or offend

Dr Lepes personally, was it about someone in particular or was it just a moment of fun? Whoever or whatever it was for, it shows that inside the damaged man, now approaching his forty-second birthday after fifteen years in prison, was a funny, rude teenager who had never quite grown up.

The second poem, called 'Sweet Maiden', and dismissively marked 'Obscene "poetry"', was more romantic, the 'obscenity' that caused the doctors to confiscate it evident only in the hopeful request of the acrostic.

> My eye is on my charming dove
> Athwart the space between our love.
> You cannot dodge me now my dear,
> Indeed you are a warming cheer.
>
> So now be good and by your smile
> Light up my hopes for a little while.
> Either be good or by your glance
> End all my hope of one small chance.
> Pretty red lips have drawn me on,
>
> Why not be like the loving swan?
> I long to fold you in my arms
> That I may feel your inner charms.
> Hark! Now and hide this rhyme away,
>
> Yet do not fail to read each day
> Or you may quite forget to dwell
> Upon the love which I would swell.

Composed by a Bug
And
Written by a Mug

July 17th Nineteen hundred and in love.

Again, there is no way of knowing to whom the poem was addressed. The 'sweet maiden' may have visited with Amelia Haswell, or have been another patient's visitor, a female employee, or even a figment of Perry's imagination. The poem suggests that, if only in his imaginings, he was still capable of passion, and that, in his imagination, he was not blind. Like the limerick it is cheeky, hinting at a brighter dimension to Perry's life in the period after Amelia Haswell's visit.

In fact, Perry had started to try to conform to the asylum rules and there seemed to be some hope that he might settle down. He had been influenced by one of the young doctors who struggled to work with this most difficult of patients in an already tough job. Amos Baker was one of the few who showed Perry real kindness. Although Amelia Haswell was ever faithful, her repeated exhortations to trust in God did little to cheer Perry. And although he repeatedly asked for news of his father and sent messages begging him to visit, Perry's own family had effectively abandoned him. The only contact he had in all his years in Dannemora was a summons from his paternal grandmother's lawyer. His grandfather had died without leaving a will and his widow, Sarah Emily, Perry's step-grandmother and aunt, was issuing summonses against all other possible claimants to the small plot of land in the Irish Settlement, including Perry. The farm itself had burned down and the land was worth about $300 in total. Dr

North was paid a fee of $1 for serving the writ that deprived Perry of his only inheritance. It was the last recorded contact Perry had with his family.

So the impact of a thoughtful doctor was considerable. His were small gestures, but they meant everything to his patient, who wrote a jaunty 'Toast to St Patrick and Dr Baker' as a thank-you when the physician had got him some pie, a favourite food. Baker arranged for him to have a water glass, an attendant's urinal, much easier for a blind man to use than a regulation chamber pot, and even some old carpet for his cold room. He also promised that he might find him a small table, so that he could eat more easily.

At last, Perry seemed to have found someone in authority he could trust. In letters to friends he wrote proudly of the 'confidence' Dr Baker reposed in him and it seemed possible that, with this encouragement, he might conform enough, by eating in his room and wearing clothes, to convince the authorities he deserved a second chance.

In the spring of 1908 that chance seemed close at hand. A letter to Dr North from Cornelius V. Collins, Superintendent of Prisons, indicated that he was convinced that Perry deserved a trial return to prison, a possible step towards eventual freedom, 'I have received the letter enclosed with your communication from Oliver Curtis Perry and am pleased to know that he shows a disposition to continue obedience to the rules. I trust you will give Oliver such personal attention as it is possible because as soon as your judgment would permit I should like to give the fellow a trial once more in the prison, as I am inclined to think that the change might benefit him temporarily at least.' Collins favoured some prison reform, and had voiced his concern that 17 per cent of prisoners had become insane. He also, coincidentally, lived in Troy and had been collared on several occasions, including once when trying to board a train, by the indomitable Amelia Haswell.

The letter that seemed to put Perry's vision of freedom within his grasp was sent on 1 April, and while it was undoubtedly genuine, it had no more effect than a cruel hoax. Two days later Collins wrote to North again: 'I have no doubt the statement relating to Perry is true in every respect. My only idea was to encourage him in every possible way to obey and respond to even a part of the institution discipline and this apparently is being done.' North had utterly rejected the idea that Perry was, or would be, fit to return to prison. Collins made another attempt to judge for himself but, as Perry commented, the doctors did little to enable their patient to make his case: 'My door was suddenly thrown open, I knew strangers were present, yet no word was spoken; so after an embarrassing silence I said, "Do you want to exhibit me like an animal or will you introduce me", Dr Mac-Donald then spoke but walked away with his visitors. I afterwards learned that they were two members of the Parole Board. Perhaps this circumstance has helped to check Mr. Collins but put yourself in my position. It is only common courtesy to speak to a convict when visitors are ushered into his presence. In my blindness I thought it was some Attendant letting a stranger steal a look at me.' The result of the 'interview' was not in Perry's favour. To add insult to injury, the bad news came in a letter from the Commissioner mistakenly addressed to the 'Hon. Curtis Perry'. The error wounded Perry, as he told his friend, because it 'puts me on a par with lunatics who are always proud of such distinctions'.

Condemned to stay in Dannemora, he found his life increasingly unbearable, although, with Baker's support, he went on trying to conform. He continued writing and even had a poem published in the *Star of Hope*. This was a remarkable prison newspaper, founded in 1899 and published by prisoners in Sing-Sing, featuring the writing of convicts across the state, that served as a means of building a sense of community as well as giving individual prisoners a voice. Perry's acrostic poem on 'Independence Day' was identified only by his prison number 'DSH 216'. Few, if any, who read the conventional patriotic verses would have known that they were written by the notorious train robber.

Perry's success encouraged him to submit another poem later the same year but his second submission, a more polemical piece, signed 'Mountain Bughouse 216', was not published. The *Star of Hope* was an invaluable voice for the prisoners of New York State, but it had to be diplomatic. Calls for reform had to be reasonable and the insane were risky allies. In the coming years they would reap little benefit from the growing efforts to treat their sane fellows with some respect.

In 1909 Amos Baker left Dannemora to take up a post at Matteawan. The repercussions were dramatic. Perry felt abandoned once again and, when some of Baker's 'concessions' were rescinded, his battle with the authorities recommenced. He soon wrote to the Reverend Warren in evident distress: 'I am now in an isolated room with two doors so that no one can hear my cries or talk to me. I defecate ['deprecate' in his transcriber's version] upon the floor in one corner and lie in the other like a wild beast.' He had been moved to the isolation cell as a punishment for what might today be called a 'dirty protest', defecating on the floor of his cell.

The protest began accidentally when the hospital sewer had

become clogged and the water closets were out of use. A blind man's sense of smell is more acute than a sighted man's, so that night, rather than use his open urinal vessel, which he could not empty until the morning, Perry defecated on some paper that he wrapped into 'a neat appearing package', and asked the night watchman to place it in the water closet. The man agreed but instead, as a cruel trick or stupid joke, slipped it back into the room. Finding it later, Perry threw it out of his window.

When he heard of the incident, a furious Dr MacDonald had Perry put in a 'north room upon the violent ward', isolated from the patients who sometimes helped him, and surrounded by a more 'irrational class of insane people'. When MacDonald also ordered that he be made to use a regulation pot, rather than the attendant's urinal Dr Baker had let him use, Perry snapped and smashed the cell window. From then on, his furniture removed as a precaution against his using it to make weapons, he defecated in his cell as a protest, as many other prisoners would do in the future, and refused to eat. He told John Warren that he was prepared to suffer any degradation rather than lose his hard-won privileges without a fight: 'I shall continue to exist just like a wild beast until they exhaust their animosity and terrorize the other patients, at which time I hope to be returned to my quarters and furnishings.'

Perry's brief truce with his keepers was over.

CHAPTER 20

'Out of His Living Tomb Speaks Oliver Curtis Perry'

OUTSIDE DANNEMORA Perry seemed to take on an almost mythical status. In 1908 *The Railroad Man's Magazine*, favoured reading of trainmen and rail fans alike, had featured his story in the latest of its series on 'Great American Train Robberies', written by Burke Jenkins. After noting the exploits of 'our redoubtable gentlemen of the road and paperbacks, the James and Younger boys', the author insisted that it 'remained for the effete East to produce what was probably the boldest railway bandit that ever existed – Oliver Perry.' The author noted that Perry was living out his days in a pitiful condition but Perry's doctors insisted on his health, strength and difficult nature, leading to a new image in the popular press, 'the Samson of Dannemora'.

Independence Day

Dannemora State Hospital 216

J ustice sails on every breeze
U nder our soldiers' flag:
L ong live the Yankees who appease
Y ou boys who do not lag!

F ollowers of our Yankee boys
O 'er mountains, vales and dales,
U nite and mingle heartfelt joys
R emote from bloodstained trails.
T o-day we see a peaceful land,
H allowed by our Savior:

N o one could find a folk more grand
I n good and square behavior.
N ational pride is soaring high,
E ach warrior shoots his guns
T hroughout the land where maidens sh̨
E 'en though they love these sons.
E very one should shout the day,
N ew vigor to inspire:

H urrah! for Uncle Sam, I say!
U nfurl the flag and fire!
N e'er cease to eulogize that soul
D estined to lead the free:
R emember how he reached the goal
E 'er sought by you and me.
D on't fail to do your very best,

A nd if the call should come,
N ot only speak but fight for rest
D espite the grapeshot's hum.

E vents have shown that we would vault
I nto a war for right,
G iving the foe no chance to halt
H owever fierce his might.
T riumphant nation! peaceful sight!

Perry's poem in the *Star of Hope*.

Perry in Dannemora.

One reporter explained the new analogy: 'Like Samson he has been shorn of the things he had, like Samson he blinded himself in his remorse, like Samson he feels about him only prison walls, like Samson he is the strongest man inside those prison walls – a veritable giant in stature and but for his sightless eyes a perfect physical specimen of manhood.' The new name was attractive, flattering even, although the extraordinary exaggeration bore little relation to Perry's actual physical stature and condition. The line-drawings in the press showed not a biblical giant but an almost classical figure, swathed in a sheet with a bandage across his eyes, looking more like blindfolded justice or Tiresias, staring blindly into a future only he could foretell.

Inside the asylum Perry was increasingly isolated from meaningful contact with the real world. He kept appealing to state officials for his case to be reviewed. Each time they had to judge the word of a criminal lunatic against that of a respected doctor, and each time the review concluded with, at best, a request that he be given a reader. He did gain some concessions, including, eventually, a ruling that a doctor be given the task of reading to him so that he no longer had to bribe a fellow patient. But, although he kept battling, some of the ties that bound him to life and other people started to break.

First his book of poetry disappeared. Although he could not

read its contents himself, it was a powerful symbol of his resistance to the grim reality of incarceration. One day, he could not find it in his cell, and nobody would tell him if it had been stolen by another inmate or confiscated. He was devastated and begged Amelia Haswell to help. She asked Dr North to have the book found because writing was therapeutic: 'I have always encouraged his composing rhyme, as I thought it would help divert his mind. . . . If I was blind and had no way of diverting my mind, I am not sure I would have a mind to divert very long.' A month later she wrote again. Perry was evidently heartbroken. Eventually North replied that even if the book was found, he would be reluctant to return it to Perry in his 'present condition'. He was in no mood to compromise.

Amelia Haswell was infuriated by Dr North's intransigence but she was even more stern with Perry who, she felt, was letting himself down. She warned him, in an eleven-page letter, that his disobedience, particularly his persistent refusal to wear clothes, condemned him in the eyes of the officials who would decide his fate. Choosing a biblical analogy, as usual, she reminded him, perhaps unwisely, of the fate of Nebuchadnezzar, 'who did not give God the glory for any of his blessings'. Might he not, she asked, rather idealistically, take his mind off his sufferings and try to do some good by influencing others? She signed off 'A Friend "in storm and sunshine"'.

But something had snapped. Perry did not read her letter: not because it was confiscated or because he had no reader, but because he refused it. His faith had always been in his Christian friends rather than in Christ, and for him God personified justice and right in this life, not the promise of eternal redemption. Now the missionary's exhortations to trust in God rang

221

hollow. He wanted to win his freedom in this life, not the next. Although her tireless support for Perry stemmed from real love and compassion, Amelia Haswell's letters are often heavy going for a reader who lacks her faith, and her model of patient suffering was one that could not have been less likely to appeal to the rebellious Perry, always more Lucifer than Christ. To Perry she was, and would remain, a friend, but her advice, always less welcome than her practical help, was now almost a torment.

Dr North lost no time in informing her that Perry was unwilling to read any more of her 'fanatical letters'. Her distress was obvious. She replied, defensively, that she was a busy woman with far too many souls to care for to spend her time working to help someone who was not willing to be helped. But, however wounded she felt, Amelia Haswell was no quitter, as she wrote: 'I cannot believe God permitted me to go through the persecution I have trying to befriend Oliver, unless some good must come from it some way, sometime, somehow.' Amelia Haswell continued to write to Oliver Perry and he later referred to her with affection, but after more than twenty years their relationship would never be quite the same.

In February 1912 another link between Perry and the world was broken. Perry had rejected his 'Mother'; now the father who had rejected him died. Oliver H. Perry slipped on a frozen sidewalk outside his home and fell, fracturing his skull. He was carried inside bleeding, as his daughter had been decades before, and died without regaining consciousness. After his death, Perry's stepmother Sarah went on to run a boarding house, while his half-brother took over their father's business. In an ironic twist, given his relatives' risky lives, Claude's son, Perry's

A letter from Amelia Haswell to Oliver Perry in 1912

nephew, became a successful insurance agent. They excised Oliver Curtis Perry from family memory.

Amelia Haswell wrote to see how Perry, who 'always seemed to have considerable affection for his father and grieved because he did not visit him', had taken the news. She wrote that Perry's attitude had always surprised her, as she knew about his rejection just when 'he needed a parent's love'.

There are of course no records of how Perry took the news, but there are signs of a change in his behaviour. Oliver H. Perry's early rejection had done irreparable damage to his son, sparking an anxiety about rejection and a compulsive need to prove himself that would contribute to his crimes and his inability to cope with prison. Perry senior's recent apparent indifference had caused him real distress. But the father's death seems to have given the son a form of release. In 1913 the reporter for *The World* who had interviewed him after the Matteawan escape was allowed to visit him and found a very different man. He was still maintaining his tough regime in protest at his conditions but now seemed to have found almost an inner calm after the repeated storms of his prison life.

Perry recognized the reporter's voice as he approached his cell and said, 'I suppose I have to make my toilet,' as the keeper unlocked his door. His 'toilet' consisted of wrapping a white band over his eyes, wrapping a towel around his loins and putting on a pair of very short prison socks. Despite the temperatures, which sometimes dropped to thirty-five below, Perry lived naked and kept the window of his room wide open day and night. 'You know,' he explained, 'I can't stand the kind of underwear they give me here. I feel very happy this way. I never catch cold. I used to suffer from colds when I was outside, but since I got rid of my clothes I am in perfect physical condition.' The report described a man who, however strange his appearance, was calm and good-humoured. He entertained his visitors by reciting his own poetry, committed to memory. The loss of his book, like the loss of his father, no longer caused him the sharp pain that had driven him to react with such self-destructive violence.

One by one he had stripped away all the trappings of his prison existence. He refused to wear the signs of his convict status, or to feel them against his skin, just as he resisted the institution's other regulations and regimes. While his self-blinding may have been a desperate return to the womb, his defiant return to an elemental state was almost a rebirth. Once the unwanted boy had sought status and comfort in the fine clothes and jewellery that he could only get through crime. Like the era he lived in, he had followed the dangerous dream of extreme individualism and material gain at any cost. Unlike the robber barons, who had bent the law with impunity, he had broken it, and lost his freedom. Now, in the brutal society of the asylum, he found another way of being, with no possessions and little respect, but a stronger sense of self-worth than he had ever had. He had turned the terrible conditions of the dungeon into a pared-to-the bone way of life.

He still hoped to be freed from Dannemora, but had accepted that he would never be seen as normal and wanted only to be sent to an asylum near his friends. The father whose love and acceptance he had never been able to win was dead and the adolescent struggles with authority, triggered by his childhood, seemed to have been played out. It is hard not to see, in the naked blind man standing in the icy wind that whistled through his cell, a fusion of raging Lear and sightless Gloucester, granted new insight through suffering.

Perry's struggle to be pardoned and sent to an asylum near his friends momentarily caught the attention of the Governor, John Dix, but, as so often happened with Perry, he seemed more fascinated by the man than his case and made no intervention.

Outside the confined world of the asylum, the free world was convulsed by conflict. The Great War raged across Europe, while the United States debated the rights and wrongs of this battle between old imperial powers. J. Pierpont Morgan lost no time in extending 500 million dollars' credit to the allied powers, but his investment in the conflict failed to raise American confidence in intervention. In New York State the battle was still being waged between those who sought to preserve the old order of patronage, particularly strong in the rural north-east, and those who argued for a regulated meritocracy to usher in a modern age of professionalism and progress. Prisons were an obvious target for both sides as numerous commissions, enquiries and investigations revealed. Accusations of financial impropriety and corruption flew to and fro in the legislature and the press, hitting reformers and conservatives alike, including Cornelius Collins who was indicted by Grand Jury for larceny and forgery. The Democratic Governor, William Sulzer, founded a 'Prison Reform Commission' that championed the ideals of the 'New Penologists', radical thinkers with ambitious ideas about what prisons could achieve. Thomas Mott Osborne embarked on his undercover operation in Auburn, exposing the horrors of the dungeon and the degradations of prison life. He and others, who had experienced the miseries of working as keepers, went on to become enlightened wardens, trying to build better regimes. There were many setbacks, but gradually some of the worst excesses of the old penal regimes were brought to light. Yet, as usual, Perry and his fellow 'patients' in what was now known as a State Hospital saw little change in their conditions.

1917 was the twenty-fifth anniversary of Perry's final train robbery. To mark it, his life story, in his own words, was published in a number of papers, melodramatically headlined by one 'Out of His Living Tomb Speaks Oliver Curtis Perry'. The story, from rejection by his parents to his robberies, self-blinding and recent protests, was a familiar one. It couched a final appeal, not for freedom, but for compassion. He knew that it was impossible to lift what he called 'the brand of insanity at this time', but was anxious to reassure those used to sensational tales of his bad, mad behaviour that he was not 'the same old Oliver Perry of years ago'. In his skill as a communicator he was very much the old Perry, pointing out the harshness of his sentence before making his appeal to be sent to a civic asylum near his old friends: 'Unless the Governor extends his humanity, I will have to serve twenty-four years and five months more, whereas a man who takes a life gets twenty years. Murderers have been in prison a dozen times before, yet they obtain a parole after twenty years of service. My simple prayer is that my sentence be reduced. The State Lunacy Commission would then have the power to transfer me to the Hudson River State Hospital at any time.'

That year America finally joined in the war that would cover the fields of France and Belgium with the graves of young men. But at the close of 1917 Perry was still to be found in his 'living tomb' at Dannemora.

He would, however, outlive the man he called his 'adversary in chief'. In December Charles North was killed by a murderer called Chris Reichert, who had been declared insane in Sing-Sing. Unlike Perry, he was judged to be no threat and made a 'trusty', so North was relaxed as he visited the carpentry workshop and talked with him about a toy he was making. But when he turned away to leave, Reichert plunged a chisel into his back. The Superintendent bled to death on the floor.

North was succeeded by his assistant, Dr John Ross, but if Perry hoped, as he so often did, that the change might be for the better, he was swiftly disappointed. Ross had a difficult task, running an ever more overcrowded and under-resourced institution. The war had made it almost impossible to recruit attendants, and, echoing Perry's 1895 assessment of the difficulty of obtaining able employees, he appealed for better pay. But nothing changed, and in the summer of 1919 he and his staff were publicly accused of maltreating their patients. The charges were identical to those repeatedly made by Perry only to be ignored, ranging from keeping inmates on an inadequate diet, 'doping' them to make them appear insane to visitors, and failing to release sane men, to causing the death of two inmates in brutal assaults by attendants. This time the complaints were voiced not by a patient, but by a lawyer whose brother was an inmate. The newly elected Democratic Governor Alfred Smith swiftly ordered a formal enquiry into conditions at the institution at which witnesses testified to harsh conditions and brutality. One ex-inmate was direct in his judgment of the Superintendent: 'Dr Ross will go the same way Dr North did. He will be killed by some one of the men. He treats men worse than dogs.'

The investigation, although welcomed by progressives, brought no radical change, and Dr Ross remained in post, while Governor Smith, a principled reformer, was caught up in a seesaw battle for New York with the sardonic Republican Nathan Miller. While Smith eventually created the Department of Corrections and transformed New York's social policy, Miller's conservatism was more in tune with the nation's intolerant, introspective post-war mood. Fear of potential enemies within, of 'reds', in the wake of the Russian Revolution, of immigrants, often assumed to be radicals, and of African Americans, who were moving north to escape continuing persecution, made it hard to work for change. The desire for 'normalcy' made it almost impossible to champion difficult causes.

In a strange synchronicity the year that Perry's chief adversary died also saw the death of his staunchest friend. On Sunday, 14 September Amelia Haswell died at the age of seventy-one. She had caught a cold that developed into pneumonia. The courageous campaigner who had risked her reputation for her principles died in the year when the women of New York were finally given the vote. She may have been naïve, even deceived by him at times, but she had been Perry's friend and champion for over thirty years. In years to come, in an ironic twist to the rumours that had dogged their relationship, she would be transformed in popular myth into his sweetheart: a pretty, but insipid, young Sunday School teacher called Amy. There is nothing in Perry's records, of which very few were preserved after the Great War, to give any hint of how he reacted to the news of Amelia Haswell's death. It is not even clear that he was told that she had died. In a sense, her death would have finally made him the orphan he had always seemed to be.

It is easy to assume that Perry was now totally alone, and he had certainly withdrawn, at least in part, from the world in which he was forced to live. But one letter, sent from the 'Natawanda Club' in New York City, suggests that he was still capable of kindness and even fun:

Dear Friend Oliva Perry, Will you please write to me and let me know if I could help you getting out of the bughouse. If you want me to get you out I will promise to do anything that is in my power. As I have friends on both side. Republicans and Democrats. Hoping to hear from you soon. As I don't forget a pal. Aspecially [sic] as slept next room as you play music aluminum bucket for two night and gave me something to eat a couple sandwiches and tobacco to chew. As I still remain your true Pal. Charles Isola.

Isola, as the reference to his politician friends implies, was a petty New York Italian gangster whose career, bound up with the new age of crime ushered in by Prohibition, had brought him briefly to Dannemora. There he had met a living embodiment of a different era of crime and the outlaw and the gangster had become friends. But his offer to help Perry never reached him. Letters from ex-prisoners had been banned.

In the aftermath of the Great War and the terrible flu epidemic that devastated the nation, political struggles continued to occupy the men charged with oversight of the most vulnerable of prisoners. In 1921, after a bitter argument, Dr Charles Pilgrim, Head of the State Hospital Commission, resigned, complaining that the Republican administration had restored 'something like pre-war conditions', while Governor Miller defended New York's 'splendid care' of the 'mentally afflicted'.

Amelia Haswell's death made it difficult for Perry to contact the press, if he wanted to, but the newspapers were filled with stories of gangland crime anyway. The new celebrity criminal was a sharp-suited gangster with a machine-gun and a moll, not a train robber with a revolver and a missionary. The few articles that appeared were grotesque, inaccurate caricatures, one describing Perry as 'an insane animal with a terrible lust for blood'. Another, in February 1924, announced 'Perry, Noted as Outlaw, Fighting Death in Prison'. The article retold the story of his past robberies, but gave no details of the threat to his life and almost no sense of his present. Perry had survived so long against the odds that he was almost an embarrassment. In an age when the stories of villains like Al Capone and clean-cut heroes like Lindbergh, the farm boy turned aviator, offered neat moral lessons, even his younger self was out of place. Perry won his fight with death, but he had been forgotten.

Four years later, after a life as quiet as Perry's had been turbulent, the other central character in the original drama bowed out. On 18 December 1928 Daniel McInerney died. That same year Governor Smith set his sights on the Presidency but lost to Republican Herbert Hoover, who confidently predicted an end to poverty. Hoover had come to public attention as the wartime head of the Food Administration, encouraging Americans to eat less with suggestions like 'Meatless Tuesdays' and 'Wheatless Wednesdays'. It is tempting to wonder what Perry might have made of his ideas. Post-war New York seemed, as it had in the Gilded Age, a glittering place of new products and unprecedented pleasures, designed now for the masses not the few. Entertainment had become a boom industry and New York was at the forefront. Country dwellers may have seen their local markets close and farmers leave their land, but a trip in a family motor car, once a sign of unattainable wealth, could take them to a picture palace.

Gloversville might not be the centre of the nation's glove-making any more, but one of its new companies, 'Shine Enterprises', ran seventy-eight picture-houses across the state, where the movie-star heroes and heroines fuelled new fantasies. Outside the walls of the Dannemora State Hospital, the unspoiled wilderness became a favourite filming location. Although the era's chronicler F. Scott Fitzgerald would call it 'the greatest, gaudiest spree in history', few realized that the spending was underpinned not by solid economic growth but by unprecedented speculation.

America was gambling with its future as Oliver Perry had done once before.

The optimistic President was worried about one growth industry: crime. Gangsters thrilled moving-picture audiences as once outlaws like Perry had gripped newspaper readers. But in reality, the prohibition of alcohol turned many ordinary men and women into petty criminals, and battling the big business of organized crime put intolerable pressure on the law enforcement agencies and the prison system. The good times had offered little to those in prison, and at the close of 1928 and in the summer of 1929, the men of Auburn and Clinton fought back against their miserable conditions in the most violent riots ever seen. Auburn was all but destroyed by fire, the Warden taken hostage, the Principal Keeper and eight prisoners killed. The riots spread across the state and beyond. Then, as order was restored in the prisons, and before the enquiry that would establish new security grading and a parole system, 24 October 1929 turned into a Black Thursday and America's great Depression began. In the Mohawk valley, men started digging for Perry's treasure, unaware that the man they thought had buried it there was still alive.

Oliver Perry died at 6.32 a.m. on 5 September 1930, just days before his sixty-fifth birthday. He had served thirty-eight years of his sentence and had spent nearly forty-five years in institutions, fighting for his freedom. The cause given on his death certificate was 'Strangulated Left Inguinal Hernia', while contributory causes were listed as an operation, conducted in the hospital three days earlier, a chronic heart infection and chronic mental condition.

The operation may have been to correct a hernia, or to remedy a different problem, such as appendicitis, inadvertently causing a hernia by cutting through the abdominal wall. No record survives and no autopsy was conducted. But in either case, weakened by decades of abuse and struggle, his body had, it seems, quite literally snapped. It is a poignant coincidence that Perry almost certainly died from the same injury that he had suffered after his dramatic chase through the snow.

The death certificate suggests almost nothing about his life. It states that his birthplace, original occupation and marital status were unknown. One statement stands out, the only suggestion that he belonged, or wanted to belong, to anyone at all: his father's name, 'Oliver H. Perry'.

Perry's death was barely noticed. One newspaper reported the passing of 'Charles Curtiss Perry', while another simply commented, 'No relatives have been located. So, Perry, inoffensive youth who turned out to be one of the most desperate bandits of his time, lies in a felon's grave.' In the press which had used him, and which he had used in return, Oliver Perry was a forgotten man: an outlaw in an age of gangsters. Nobody thought to dramatize his story as they would those of the outlaws he was judged to have 'outdone': in the cinemas, the new tales of the Old West had no place for a New Yorker, no matter how daring his crimes. But Oliver Perry had, and has, an afterlife.

In the hospital itself, he left such an impression that attendants who first worked there years after his death swore they had known 'Old Blind-Eye Perry'. In the stories of his daring crimes that sent Depression-era treasure-seekers out to dig for gold in the hills, in the careful narratives by railroad aficionados, in cartoons and in bedtime stories, traces of Perry survived.

Fittingly, his name has also been written into the landscape of the Mohawk valley near the site of his first robbery. Although the hunt for his treasure has ended, boys and girls in Utica still know of a special place to go, to be alone, to hide, to get away. It is one of those exciting but scary places that become the landmarks of remembered childhood. 'Perry's Cave', where he hid after the robbery, is now the only physical memorial to a man who was once one of America's most notorious, most wanted men: Oliver Curtis Perry.

I PUT OFF visiting the Dannemora graveyard for a long time. While I was looking for Oliver Perry, I didn't want to see his grave. Eventually, feeling that I had to, I wrote to the prison authorities and asked if I might visit it and take a photograph. After some negotiation they agreed, but warned me that it would not be easy to find. There are no names on the gravestones of men who died in the Dannemora State Hospital, only numbers, those allotted when they entered the institution. I reminded myself that it was probably a matter of confidentiality, or economy, rather than indifference. But there was something terrible about the fact that these men, cut off for so long from family and society, should, in the end, still have only institutional identities.

The graveyard for Clinton prison is by the main road, easily accessible to visitors. The final resting place of the prisoners judged insane is, as they were, hidden from public view. Their bodies could be claimed for private burial, but those whose families could not, or would not, come for them were interred in a remote part of the grounds. It occurred to me as I drove with a prison official from the hospital buildings, past the prison farm to the edge of the forest that sweeps up the mountainside, that I was one of very few people who had visited the graves of these unwanted men. I thought of Perry asking to be buried 'alongside dear Blanchy', and of the respectable monument, standing tall in the Syracuse cemetery, that now holds all the family but one.

We passed a small area designated as the Jewish burial ground, then continued on foot across rougher terrain. My guide was friendly and apologetic. They had been trying, he explained, to restore the prison graveyards and had made good progress with the main cemetery. But this one, in a fitting parallel to the history of New York's prison reform, was the last to be renovated. We walked to a sloping field of scrubby grass, where the roots of fir trees tangled across stones the size of house bricks. This was the graveyard. Some of the grass had recently been cut, possibly for my visit, and I could just about discern that the stones were in rows, but only a dozen or so were visible, standing a few inches clear of the earth. These were the graves of the unclaimed men. I had spent years searching for Perry and now I was looking again. I rubbed the earth from half-submerged stones and peered to decipher numbers eroded by decades of rain and ice. But there was no sign of 216.

On the slope above the stones, under tree roots that have gradually snaked downwards, and soil carried by spring mud-slides as the snows of winter melt, lie more graves. There men buried by the guards have been buried again, and the stones, the markers of their prison identities, covered over. As I wiped the earth from my hands and walked among the tangled roots, I suddenly found myself smiling. For a man who had fought the system so ferociously that he sacrificed his own body and mind to have been found, finally, in an allocated plot, identified for ever by his prison number, would have seemed like defeat. Instead his body has been covered by the wildness of nature as it reclaims the land from the state. Perry has escaped one last time.

It seemed a fitting, and open, conclusion to my search. Just as his boyhood home had disappeared, enveloped in the broadleaf woodland of the Mohawk valley, so his grave had been subsumed within the darker forest of the Adirondacks. The traces of his life that I had found in the years of looking had brought me closer to him than I had ever expected, but he was still out of reach. The daring robber I had set out to find turned out to be America's broken dream boy, an unwanted child determined to make his mark in a society whose passions and problems he epitomized. His daring crimes that had first caught my eye had made him an instant celebrity, but it was his long struggle to survive, to preserve his identity in a system designed to reduce him to a number that had commanded my respect. I had found the courage, strength and spirit that I had looked for in an outlaw lover, riding free across the Western landscape of my fantasy, in a man who was confined in institutions almost all his life. And looking for the man of my dreams had changed me.

Instead of restoring my imagined scene of childhood innocence, or transporting me into a romantic fantasy, my search had taken me into a darker, harsher world. But there I encountered someone with more determination to savour even life's bitter pleasures than I could have imagined. In the years after I first saw his picture, Oliver Perry had charmed, shocked, infuriated and moved me, as he had the men and women he encountered in his lifetime. In my research I had tried my best, as they had, to pin him down. At times I came quite close to knowing something of what, and who, he was. I saw him at his best and at his worst. But he always escaped. I could never make him mine. And, in the end, I was glad that I could not.

In my strange relationship with Oliver Perry I learned that no matter how much we yearn to belong, to possess and be possessed by anyone, parent, forbidden sweetheart or wanted man, in the end we are alone. When we are children and when we are grown, our desires must always leave us wanting.

Acknowledgements

I COULD FILL another book with the names of all the people who have helped in my search for Oliver Perry and in my efforts to tell his story. These acknowledgements are only a suggestion of my gratitude to them all. While it feels like a minor betrayal of Perry's memory, I must first thank the Department of Correctional Services of the State of New York, especially Superintendents William Mazzuca, Daniel Senkowski and Hans Walker, Deputy Superintendents Paul Annatts and Jimmie Harris, Plant Superintendent Dale Gordon, Lt G. Wilkerson, Faculty Historian Michael Pettigrass, Correction Officer Michael O'Sullivan and Dr Leonard I. Morgenbesser. Whatever happened in the past, the current representatives of New York's Correctional Services could not have been more courteous or helpful. I would also like to thank the staff of the New York State Archives, especially Dr William Evans and Dr James Folts, who helped me locate Perry's records and writings. Dr John R. Sellers and Mrs Nan Ernst, of the Library of Congress, kindly allowed me to work with the Pinkerton National Detective Agency archive before cataloguing.

The following individuals, in New York and further afield, all gave me invaluable help and encouragement: Rebekah Ambrose, Peter Bedrossian, Joe Bendle, Ruby Biswas, Michael V. Carlisle, Doreen Chaky, Beverly Choltco-Devlin, Dorothea Cooper, Phil Cubbin, Barbara Dix, Thomas G. Eldred, Andi Evangelist, Deborah J. Ferrell, Carlton Gilroy, Malcolm Goodelle, Hope V. Hatch, Edward Knoblauch, Virginia LaGoy, Michael Martin, Nancy Martin, Eileen McHugh, Rick Miller and the National Association for Outlaw and Lawman History, Sharon O'Brien, Roy O'Dell, Jeanette Shiel, Tom McCarthy of the New York Correctional History Society, Wayne Miller of the Feinberg Library, Joan Van Voorhis, Paul Paciello, Richard Palmer, Emma Parry, Joe Price, Mat Rapacz, Ruth Rosenberg-Naparsteck, Wendy Scalfaro, Joe Sim, Daniel Smith, Debra Staley, Gina Stankivitz, and Kelly Yacobucci-Farquahar. I would also like to thank colleagues and students, too many to list, at Liverpool John Moores University for their support and suggestions.

I have very special memories of my research in upstate New York because of the good company, hospitality and kindness of Mark de Lawyer, Dawn Capece, Marta Zimmerman, Larry-Ann Evans, Robert Weiss and Ann Rowland and David. Without the enthusiasm and encouragement of James Friel and Peter Wheeler, the passionate advocacy of Jane Turnbull, and the skill and sensitivity of Alexandra Pringle, Chiki Sarkar and their colleagues at Bloomsbury, my obsession with Oliver Perry would have remained a private matter.

Tamsin Spargo was born and raised in Cornwall. She worked as a reporter, then as an actor, before embarking on her current career as a cultural historian. She is Reader in Cultural History and Director of the School of Media, Critical and Creative Arts at Liverpool John Moores University. Her academic works include *The Writing of John Bunyan*, *Foucault and Queer Theory* and *Reading the Past: Literature and History*.

A NOTE ON THE TYPE

The text of this book is set in Linotype
Sabon, named after the type founder,
Jacques Sabon. It was designed by Jan
Tschichold and jointly developed by
Linotype, Monotype and Stempel, in
response to a need for a typeface to be
available in identical form for mechanical
hot metal composition and hand
composition using foundry type.

Tschichold based his design for Sabon
roman on a font engraved by Garamond,
and Sabon italic on a font by Granjon. It
was first used in 1966 and has proved an
enduring modern classic.